EIGHT SEASONS

walking in rhythm with nature

EIGHT SEASONS

Copyright © 2023 by Alison SMITH

First Edition

ISBN 978-1-7384218-3-1

Prepared by TGH International Ltd.

www.TGHBooks.com

EIGHT SEASONS

walking in rhythm with nature

ALISON SMITH

This is dedicated to my family from before, my family ahead, and those who I chose, and chose me, as family.

That means you.

"You and I walk on this earth together and see her beauty every moment."

Disclaimer/Advisory

Each person has free will and can decide if and when to make choices relevant to their forward movement through life. Please be aware that ideas in this book are suggestions for entertainment purposes only.

Safety of your own individual body, mind & spirit is your responsibility to ensure at all times.

Contents

introduction

I'm an astrologer who doesn't believe in time.

At least not time as we use it today.

When we watch the stars, the Sun, and the Moon, it is to touch something more than we can ever know. By standing on our earth, we have our unique perspective of looking outwards at the horizon, the sky above, our lives, and how they will turn out. The Earth turns and moves through space, and we are held in place by gravity. The Universe conjures up different energy patterns formed by the movements of Earth, the Sun, and Moon, other planets, and ourselves; every moment is unique - never to be repeated.

Let me repeat that for you - every single moment that we experience (and those that others experience) are stand-alone breathtaking magical moments in this Universe of ours.

Hope.

This is a book of hope and to inspire remembering why we are here … on Earth.

If you wonder why you're here and want to know more about how you fit in, this book is for you. We really do all fit in here and always have done and always will. However, it is also our role, or maybe a part of our role, to evolve and give ourselves permission to do that. And we have a responsibility to those who came before us and to those who will follow. If we think about the connection we have to our grandparents' grandparents and then forward to our grandchildren's grandchildren, we begin to see just how we fit into this life of ours and yet also have an unbroken responsibility to grow for ourselves and our home planet. And, if you believe that the time/energy fields are neither linear nor our version of logic as I do, then it follows that our thoughts and actions also affect the Universe in our past, present, and future.

Recycling our coffee cups whilst meditating once a week is not enough - and if you believe that too, then you're in the right place!

Whilst you may not, like me, have been blessed to have given birth to children in this lifetime, we all have the same connection to each other and to what will become our legacy. We need to leave this home in the same way as when we arrived. Think of it as if it is a house move. We would clean, tidy, and make ready for the next occupants to enjoy. And, no doubt, with all of the significant enhancements we have given our old home whilst we lived there.

So it is with this lifetime of ours. We grow and expand our

understanding of life; the cycle of life flows around us and through us, and the vibrations travel onwards.

There is a remembering of where we are in the life cycle of ourselves and those around us. The living beings with which we share this planet have their own pulse and rhythm inside the cycle of life, from the microbes in our soil with duties of breaking down plant matter to the birds in the sky transporting seeds from place to place - everything and everyone with their roles to play in our quest to evolve.

And that's what this book has at its heartbeat. The quest is to evolve ourselves and our planet and remember our ancestors and what they can teach us. And then to take those lessons and expand them as we, too, grow and explore.

You may already know that my 'day job' is working as an astrologer, intuitive, and author. I've worked professionally for more than 30 years, giving talks, leading workshops, presenting group programs, and reading astrological charts all over the UK. Plus, I've appeared in magazines and on local radio stations. During that time, I've also taught Tarot and symbolism and how to walk within the seasons of the year. The practical ways of living on this earth and using the energies all around us to make OUR best way through life.

We are all unique and have our own different connections with this amazing planet Earth and the Universe. And yes - I'm also known as a very Practical Astrologer! You'll see, I hope, through this book that I love our choices for what we do and when we do it. Watching the movement of the stars and their offered energies gives us our best choices to make.

I will add that nothing is fated or absolute destiny, as we all have free will and decide our choices through life!

Magic.

Listening to our connection with the Earth and the stars, truly hearing our own inner language, and acting upon those nudges that are meant to be guiding gives us information about where our best choices may be and permission to be so much more ...

Are you ready to live in the flow of life? To delve deeply and reach upwards to create a space of connection? Sometimes, the most natural of perspectives are the simplest and also the most significant, and by deeply experiencing life through the natural rhythm of nature, we hear those choices for us and our planet even more loudly!

How amazing is that!!

the natural wheel of the year

Nature holds everything we need. Everything! From the basic building blocks of our lives and warmth, water, food, and the ability to make shelters through to giving us clues at every moment and every turn of what we can do to make this world, and our lives, even more glorious. And the first, most obvious, nudge about how we live more centred and connected is through the cycle of the seasons - nature showing us the way forward in her finest role.

Spring, Summer, Autumn, and Winter have a natural rhythm to them that, when we align or re-align ourselves with it, gives us all of the symbolism possible for loving our lives. And these seasons are not a random display of heat and cold gifted by the sky. The movement of Earth and the Sun and Moon determines when the seasons change, and so our rhythm of agriculture follows. And celebrations ... did I mention this is a book of celebration? Our ancestors noted and marked every turn of the season as important moments in their calendars.

Knowing when to plant, harvest, and rest the fields is important information for allowing food to be available throughout the year.

And there is a regularity to the seasons which would have been noticed back in the depths of time. It's a subtle nuance of being more than the four seasons. We cannot know exactly when the eight seasons began to be watched and observed; however, we can look back in the history of many countries and ancient civilisations to see this in place.

The movements of the stars were watched avidly for what they may herald. Our perception of the Sun moving through the constellations was one of the earliest mysteries explored as planetary movements were monitored (such as they could be seen by eyes only!) together with weather patterns and fluctuating temperatures so a picture would begin to emerge of the natural cycle we could use, and use very effectively, for crop growing, travel, and development.

Perhaps the most dramatic, and waited for, are the two moments when the Sun appears to stand still and then leads us into the next half of the year - either darker or lighter.

Winter Solstice & Summer Solstice are THE moments when the Earth changes our seasons into, respectively, the lighter half of the year and a darker half. The shortest or longest day offers a shift into a different world, almost with the certain knowledge that we will need to live our lives differently. The term 'Solstice' literally means the sun stands still and, whilst nothing actually does ever stand still (or move backwards for that matter - more about this later!), this is a pivot time for the Earth and a shake-up that is ... a complete change of season! Of course, there are also the two moments when light and dark are equal - the equinoxes of Spring and Autumn.

However, there are also four other festivals, lesser known but still so important, and they are what we call the cross-quarter festivals because they are at quarters to the four already mentioned.

These are Imbolc, Beltane, Lammas and Samhain/Halloween - also known as the Power Festivals!

So let's put these into order, and you will begin to see how everything fits together:

Winter Solstice;
Imbolc;
Spring Equinox;
Beltane;
Summer Solstice;
Lammas;
Autumn Equinox;
Samhain;

And then the cycle begins again with Winter Solstice ...

These are all solar festivals and determined, both astrologically and for agricultural purposes, by the Sun. And, as I've already mentioned, it's so useful to know where we are in the year for growing, harvesting, travelling and resting - both for us and the ground! Mythology, stories, watching the Sun & Moon, taking actions at the best of times, philosophically pondering - all of this helps us to remember our place here on earth and our position in the cycle of evolution.

I began to write this book at a Winter Solstice with the intention of us walking together through old and new ways of aligning ourselves with the natural turn of our planet ... the wheel of the year ...

Winter Solstice. The time when the Sun 'returns' to the sky and brings hope.

Winter is both a challenging season and a beautiful one. A time of bright lights, colours, gifts and love. It's also a season for looking backwards, acknowledging losses and keeping an eye on our resources of food, warmth and shelter. And our Universe begins to show us lengthening days and the faintest glimpse of greenery appearing around us.

You may begin to read the book at any point in the cycle of the Sun through our sky. You may follow along with the seasons, or your ancestors will speak to you; mine do regularly (!) and show you their own pathways for your musing. Just start - in this book we recognise our uniqueness!

growing flax

I've spent years (probably many lifetimes) watching the seasons and doing different things to fully appreciate the life cycle of nature and our planet. As this book was being dreamt, I immersed myself in a project to grow flax.

The history of flax growing is an interesting one, with records showing this useful crop being produced as far back in time as Ancient Egyptian and, at times, was the most prolific crop grown. Its uses are varied, with the seeds used for oil and food together with the fibres used for linen and thread.

However, it is a slow-growing, labour-intensive crop and needs a lot of space to produce enough yarn to make a square of cloth.

And that is where the real heart of this book exists.

Our ancestors grew flax to produce cloth for ... sails for ships, cloth to sell, a dress to wear ... No wonder they darned holes in socks and clothing - cloth was a precious article!

There will be more about this throughout the book; however, just for a moment, look at the textiles around you and begin to touch in with your ancestors and the lengths they would go to to make or acquire clothing, bed linen, rugs ...

time & calendars

Using clocks and watches is a relatively new method of keeping time. Not many generations ago, the passage of the Sun would have given us a sense of where we were in the day. Waking at sunrise and sleeping after sunset is a natural way of ensuring we make the most of daylight and warmth from the Sun.

And there is more. By living inside the seasons, the cycles and rhythms of the year, our ancestors could use the rhythm of the Sun to grow crops and plan for travel and socialising.

The Gregorian calendar was introduced during the 16th Century, and although there are other calendars used throughout our world, it is the most popularly used.

But ... it is relatively modern, and we rely on adding in an extra day every four years to cope with the progress of the Sun. The Sun, the Moon, and other planets just don't conform to our concept of clocks and calendars!

the sun & the moon

The Sun is our star. It is by the earth's position in relation to the Sun that we know the time of day and the season of the year. And so, if we consider this celestial body for a moment and appreciate that the Sun is a star that constantly burns in the sky, then it follows that it sends us light and heat for our planet Earth to have life.

Take a look around you outside at nature right this moment:

What is growing? Or not growing?

Can you see the Moon at night, and what does she look like?

So, how do we know what's happening if we don't monitor the sky? A good ephemeris (a timetable of the stars if you like!) will list out year by year, day by day, the exact day/time that certain stars & planets will appear in a zodiac sign. The Sun entering a new constellation (from our perspective) may be from the 19th through to the 23rd of a month. Remember that the Universe does not dance to our calendar but rather has its own tune!

By the way, and I'll introduce astrology along our way, there is no such thing as a planet being on a cusp and so 'of' two zodiac signs simultaneously. A star/planet will always be in one zodiac (constellation) sign or another, and this will vary from year to year. By consulting an ephemeris, we find the exact day/time. Was the Sun at the end or the very beginning of a sign of the zodiac when you were born? Unsure about your zodiac sign? A reputable astrologer will be able to work it out, given your date of birth and year!

And now, we begin to consider the cycle and rhythm of the moon, from the sliver of light that is the New Moon through the growing towards fullness—then diminishing energy and light to the darkest of the cycle before the next new moon. The Moon has no light of her own and reflects light from the Sun. The amount of moonlight that we 'see' shows us the phase of the moon.

A New Moon astrologically is in the same sign of the zodiac as the Sun and occupies the same part of the sky. The light grows as the Moon separates away from the Sun.

Full Moon astrologically is in the opposite sign of the zodiac as the Sun, and these two celestial bodies are opposite each other at that time. Moonlight is at the fullest, maximum beam, reflecting the full amount of light from the Sun.

If you haven't already, please go outside and look at the Moon.

Sarah, a client, once wrote to me that she only went outside to gaze at the night sky because I said to do so in a social media post. 'I can't believe I'd forgotten to do that. I was only outside for a short while but felt the presence of the universe all around me.'

Next time you go outside to moon gaze, remember to sense the enormity and the potential of our wonder-full Universe!

how to use this book

There is a power and a usefulness in observing the cycles &
rhythms of the earth and our universe, for the key to how we
'fit' in! And even more information about our belonging in
this Universal system of ours is the observance of those eight
seasons of the year.

Through the seasons of Imbolc and Little Spring into Spring
proper. Then, the beginning of ripening into the height
of Summer. Seeing what will be harvested, or useful, into
recognising what there is for the darker months and then
beginning to retreat into the ground ready for rest.

The knowledge that the basic building blocks of life itself
depended on each season isn't buried so far away in our lives
today - even with our dependance on electricity. We can
remember and begin to align ourselves into this most natural of
rhythms. This is the real alchemy of existence and how we find
our own philosopher's golden stone.

However you approach this book, and whichever season of the year you begin it in, you will find ideas, magic, alchemy and:

- **Being** - history & symbolism
- **Doing** - where plants are in their journey and listening to our inner world
- **Playing** - how to celebrate and interact with nature
- **Stillness** - the listening and hearing our planet Earth

And, because our ancestors watched the stars to make sense of what was happening for them day by day, there are some astrological insights along the way. Your birth chart, the moment of arrival here on Earth, is made up of a snapshot of the Universe for your first breathe here on Earth. Your map of the stars has all of the twelve signs of the zodiac, planet, and star energies for your use.

We are all wired into the natural pulse of the Universe by a) living here on Earth, b) having a unique pattern of stars within constellations for our moment of birth, and c) being in an unbroken lineage of those who have come before us and those who will live after!

How we learn comes from many different directions, and Nature herself is our greatest teacher. From books and films, we absorb history presented from other opinions and thoughts. During our childhood, we will have taken on board perceptions and stories as well as the subject learning inside schools, etc. Our past and future ancestors also have much to show us about life and living. In this book, I've included 'Notes from the

Ancestors' as another way of tuning our frequencies to as many thought processes as possible - some will resonate for you, and some will not! And that is what is so amazingly wonderful about the uniqueness of every single one of us. We are all different, yet we are creating a whole being living on planet Earth and preparing the road forward!

We live our lives forward (yes, absolutely forward!), and whether we observe a particular 'planetary shift' or not, we still move forward. That is why this book will offer suggestions for each season, and please choose which resonates - and even introduce your own! You're here, in my world, and so I know you're curious!

I'm writing this from my home in the Northern Hemisphere. And the seasons, for me, flow through cold Winters and warmer Summers with a natural menu of things to do to both celebrate and use the energies available. If you live in a different part of the world, the seasons will have the same rhythm but at different times. Remember that Winter Solstice for one half of the planet becomes Summer Solstice for the other. Admittedly, there are places on our Earth where the sun never rises (or only for a very short time), so the notion of seasons based on 'half a planet' may not be technically correct.

However, by observing the seasons of the year as they flow, by walking with the natural rhythm of the planet, we find our own natural flow. Life itself becomes easier as we connect our bodies to the natural rhythms of our planet, and it will also help us make sense of what is going on around us. It's like plugging ourselves into the biggest, and at times most mysterious, circuit board there is!

Together, if you join me, we will see just how each and every one of us has a role to play in the next few thousand years!

Now go to the season you resonate with …

And, as always, with love from Alison

yule

Winter Solstice /
Yule

Halloween/
Samhain

Imbolc

Autumn Equinox /
Harvest

Spring Equinox /
Ostara

Lammas /
Harvest

Beltane /
May Day

Summer Solstice /
Midsummer

yule - december & january

Our season of Yule begins at the Winter Solstice and will take us through days when we subtly begin to see more light.

Is there a glimmer of returning warmth? Might the ground begin to be fertile again? Is there hope? Hope for the year ahead?

By observing the moment the Sun enters the zodiac sign of Capricorn, around the 21st of December, we witness one of the best mysteries created for us - the Sun begins to give us more light!

Known as the festival of Yule (although other names are also, and have been, used), this season will last from the Winter Solstice until the festival of Imbolc at the beginning of February. The Yule wreaths on our front doors represent the unbroken wheel of the year, and there is deep symbolism in how these are often made. Holly with red berries representing the vitality of life, perhaps of our lifeblood. Mistletoe offers the gift of freedom and new passions ahead - where will that kiss under the mistletoe, or your dreams, take you? And pine cones, bearers of seeds, hold the promise of new lives and new beginnings to emerge.

The season of Yule isn't only about one calendar date, though, as it holds moments for amazing shifts as our home planet travels through Space. Together, we are going to explore those exact points of shifting into the different seasons - the planetary rhythms that living here on planet Earth offers us as our own natural cycle through life. But to do that, we need to know how to listen, hear and be in the BE-ING of Human Beings.

Before we begin to explore more of this season, please take a moment to *BE* ...

grounding & connnecting

Take a moment right now to sense where you are by standing (or sitting) still.

There is no need to close your eyes or schedule this in your diary - take a moment to reach your awareness down to the ground beneath your feet.

Plant yourself on the earth and, if you feel inclined, stamp your feet gently to remind your body where you are.

Connected to the Earth.

And then expand this moment of connection by reminding yourself of the sky above your head and how the universe stretches out to infinity.

Connected to the Earth and the Universe.

This is the fastest way I've ever found that we can ground ourselves when feeling ... well ... ungrounded! Try it the next time you're waiting for a bus for a moment or two and observe how instantly plugged into living here on earth you feel!

Tuning into the Earth and the Universe.

It really is as simple as this.

Use your moment to be aware of the Earth beneath your feet and the sky above your head.

Feel the horizon of our planet stretching out from either side of you and in front and behind.

And now you are grounded and tuned in to your own connection with the Universe itself - magical!!

winter solstice

The seeds under the ground have
everything they need

...

Winter solstice is the shortest day of the year and the day that's the turning point of the year. It marks the end of the dark half of the year and the beginning of the growing part of the year. And it's those moments of asking the Sun to return which is so crucial to the celebrations that we find throughout this period of time. Our ancestors would have been so much more in tune with what's going on for the planet and beyond. Every sunbeam, every drop of rain, every turn of the soil was crucial to life itself. It was necessary for crops. It was needed for safe travel. It showed whether there was enough food to last through the really darkest days of winter for whoever was under our roof at the time.

The notion of the Sun appearing to lengthen our days and give us more light and more warmth just when necessary was absolutely crucial to everything we know. Think for a moment of life before refrigerators, before electric lights and travel by cars. It was only by the light of the Sun and the light of the Moon that we could actually travel.

The point of exact Winter Solstice (or Summer Solstice for December if you're in the southern hemisphere) is when the Sun moves from the zodiac sign of Sagittarius and into Capricorn. And all of us are able to feel that shift occur (if we wish to) as it connects to each of our birth charts. Remember that when we're born, the map of the stars all around us is unique and holds energy from all of the stars and all of the constellations! Therefore, our connection with the stars right now, this very moment, is different for each of us as the stars align with our birth chart.

The concept of planets and stars having special energy unique to each of them is something built up over a thousand years or more of observations, mythology, curiosity and research. In this book, you'll meet some of the gods and goddesses who, through their myths and stories, have fleshed out planetary energy in order for us to choose which we use. I'll offer you different ways of looking at the stars, and some will resonate and others not. All I ask is that you consider the different ways of looking at the energy offered by each constellation/sign of the zodiac, each star and planet and how we can interpret the energies when blended and connected to us on Earth. Picture the planetary energies beaming towards us from within the constellations like an artist's pallet of beautiful oil paints available to us at any moment in time!

The Sun moving into Capricorn heralding Winter Solstice will occur around the 20th - 23rd of December - a good ephemeris, or decent search on the internet, will tell exactly when year by year this happens. And Capricorn is, in my experience, the most driven, beautiful and ambitious part of the zodiac. Capricorn is ruled by Saturn, also known as the great timekeeper, which seems extremely fitting for this time of the year. Saturn rules work and offers golden rewards for those who step up to their challenges and take the steps necessary to move forward or, perhaps, inspire others to do so.

Saturn in Capricorn loves to celebrate
(yes, really!) life itself.

At this time of the year, still in the depths of cold and dark, the energy all around feels sluggish and 'beneath the surface.' And yet, nothing is ever stopped in our cycle of life, and so perhaps we try to see the cold and dark as protective. We only go outside when we need to do something such as work, shop for food or, as our ancestors would, collect firewood.

The earth itself is protecting seeds and animals in hibernation. We think more about our layers of clothing to wear and feel amazing when we go for a brisk walk in the cold. It's a time to get our bodies in sync with the season by dressing in warm clothing and planning how we will venture out. It is much easier with heaters in our cars and buses, but we still have to consciously consider whether ice is on the ground and how we will get to our vehicles. Food such as soup warms us through and through - quick to make with just a few vegetables and herbs. Holding a bowl of steaming soup brings a sense of joy to our souls and, perhaps, brings memories to the surface.

Yule is a season of protection,
warmth, thoughtfulness and one step at a time.

And so, at the end of December, there's still snow and yes, we'd still be relying on whatever preserved meat and vegetables were in our stores.

But ... you know ... the human spirit wants to survive.

We actually want hope, and we want
to see that there are better times ahead.

festivals & 'ho' to the sun

There are so many festivals at this particular time of the year and, I'm sure you will find others but let's think of just a few:

Hanukkah is the eight-day Jewish festival of lights. It can occur between mid-November and late December and is determined by the Hebrew calendar. It is also called the Festival of Dreams and features a candle lit each evening until all eight are beaming their light out.

Christmas Day, with the celebration of the birth of Jesus, is followed by *Boxing Day*, and this was a day when Christmas boxes, usually gifts of money, were given out to people experiencing poverty and, in later years, tradespeople.

Hogmanay is celebrated hugely in Scotland with the bells ringing in the next new year, and traditions abound! It's believed that the first person entering the house after the bells have rung will either bring joy or misfortune and, often, a friend or family member will be sent out of the home just before the new year is sounded to be the 'first-footer' across the threshold! This would ensure good fortune for the year ahead, with even more luck to come if the first visitor has with them coins, a lump of coal or whisky.

All of the festivals at this time of the year are devoted to the hope of light returning.

Hope for the Sun and life itself returning.

Hope for light.

Hope for the continuance of the cycle of life.

Hope for growth.

ancient romans & the festival of saturnalia

The Romans celebrated Saturnalia (by the way, as Saturn rules Capricorn, it isn't such a random name!) for a whole month at this time. Feasting, celebrating, dancing and the reversal of roles featured heavily in this festival for them. In a reversal of roles, the lords served the servants and monies (or seeds) given out to those who had served during the year. They were responsible for the early transportation of ginger, and it's very symbolic as a spice still used by us to create gingerbread houses. We make food to bring warmth to our hearth and home.

And the symbolism of that echoes through the ages ...

Records seem to indicate that the Romans were the first to put cloves into oranges and, again, this is symbolic of ensuring richness and the best of food for the months to come - plus, of course, the scents were most likely very welcome inside homes that had been enclosed for several months with people, and livestock, living next to each other keeping warm!

Saturnalia began mid-December and went through until mid-January and, as far as we know, completely focussed on feasting and celebrating. By having feasts at this time, they were saying that their tables would be full for the next year and encouraging the attraction of abundance. And so, too, can we join in this! Bring on the abundance for the month to come.

In the Celtic world, we had our own tale of mystery for this time, and that is the story of the Oak King and the Holly King.

oak king & holly king

The story goes (origin lost in the mists of time) of the battle between the Oak King and the Holly King at the Solstice times.

Two kings ruled for a half year each. There is only one crown, and so, twice a year, the battle ensues between the strong Oak King, who campaigns to inspire passionate growth and the evergreen Holly King, who brings stability and greenery in the face of dire circumstances.

Who will wear the crown?
When will the Sun return?

The Sun stands still and prepares to move from the zodiac sign of Sagittarius (the archer) and into the sign of Capricorn (the goat). The battle commences for the winner of this battle to wear the crown and rule for a full six months.

In December, and in our Northern Hemisphere, the Oak King is determined to win over the Holly King, who has worn the crown since June. After a keenly fought battle, the Oak king is triumphant! He will wear the crown adorned with acorns for the growing half of the year. The Sun is returning to the sky, and light will grow more day by day. The newly crowned Oak King becomes the beacon of hope as the Sun begins to warm the soil. The pathway ahead clears and is ready for our walk forward into the new cycle of growth.

Capricorn's zodiac energy begins,
and the people all around can rejoice.

However …

Often, snow is still on the ground, providing a white carpet and making travel difficult. It's impossible to rapidly move 'out there', yet there is still time for letting the new energy, ideas, thoughts and musings gently percolate within.

Seeds beneath the soil, and of course, the acorns, have everything they need to be inspired into life growth - the correct nutrients, moisture, and the will to grow are all in place … they have to wait for the best of times. Nothing is resting at this time. Life is beginning to consider when to emerge.

gregorian calendar

How about the significance of the Gregorian Calendar and
its emphasis on the year beginning on January 1st? I have
an argument for a different 'year start', and it's not about a
particular date but rather more of a seasonal nudge into new
growth ... however, as we all need some form of calendar
to work and synchronise our appointments and such,
standardisation does become necessary!

The Gregorian calendar has only been in use for around 300
years, and before that, the Julian Calendar was in place for
about 1,600 years. We can look back in history and see many
different calendars have been tried and used to bring some form
of order to the 'days' although none (even back as far as Mayan
times) are able to cope with the way that our Earth dances with
the Sun and the Moon.

Adding a day every four years is nothing new - we have a history of needing to alter calendars stretching back as far as records begin.

Try looking at the times of sunrise and sunset to have a feel of how our ancestors would have, for thousands of years, viewed their waking and sleeping patterns.

And then watch how certain dates are used and misused, usually for reasons of commerce.

to focus on hope

What about that wave of hope that circles the earth at this time? Would you add colour and music to touch with just how crucial the warmth returning was for your ancestors?

Pine, Spruce, Holly and Bay leaves are all amazing examples of evergreen plants and trees with foliage that stays green beyond the usual growing seasons. Bringing greenery into the home is an ancient tradition of connecting and remembering growth. There are uplifting scents from most evergreen leaves, too, which would have been welcome inside homes which had to be closed to the outside elements for several months. And so, by having a green tree in our home, a holly wreath on our door and even bowls of nuts on our table, we symbolise the hope associated with the turning wheel of the year.

There are different ways to mark the days after the Solstice and perhaps remind ourselves that the days are becoming brighter!

We have a tradition in our household of giving a small gift on Winter solstice and then for 11 more evenings.

Twelfth night is recognised in the Christian calendar as Epiphany and one of the most important feast days, usually falling on the 6th of January.

Watching the New Moon in the sign of Capricorn, together with the astrology around the Solstice, will give us ideas of how we will move through the new seasons. Take a look at your birth chart, if you have it drawn up, and see how the Sun moving through Capricorn will offer you extra possibilities. Or go for a walk through the forest at this time and find a tree to touch and maybe just maybe, the spirit of the Oak King will whisper words to you!

ground-breaking news!

The first Monday after festivities have concluded, and noticing when the ground was ready, was called Plough Monday by our ancestors and had its own ritual of new beginnings. There would have been such a joy with the snow receding; soil could be turned over to make ready for planting, and plans could be made. Early planting meant crops ready sooner and food for humans and animals, and news of 'Plough Monday' would spread like wildfires with the implications of the start of inspiring new growth to come.

And with that first turn of the plough, or spade in the ground, came the responsibility for planting what was needed and would grow during the year ahead.

It's useful to think about the 'No Dig' method, which has had a resurgence over the past few years and will, no doubt, expand more. Especially favoured by organic food producers, as well as gardeners, it doesn't alter the ecosystem of our soil.

Instead of digging up weeds and turning the soil, the plants are allowed to die back naturally, and fallen leaves remain where they are. Compost, or other manure, is spread on top of the soil to allow old plants, bugs and worms to break down all of the organic matter and bring it into the 'whole' of the soil.

The natural ecosystem is undisturbed, and the planting of new seeds takes place in soil which has been, by and large, prepared by Nature herself!

our purposeful living

These ideas are just that, 'ideas', but they also help move us through this season. Feel free to evolve them and add your own. Every time I've introduced people to walking with the rhythm of the Earth, they have found the 'new old' and 'new new' ways of living the cycle. Each season offers us different energies to be used in a myriad of ways. The joy of being human is that we choose what we do and when to celebrate and attract the best of turns of the wheel for ourselves and our planet.

The astrology around every moment is different and yet has themes based on the Solar cycle, and that is what can make our practices of 'Being, Doing, Playing & Stillness' so unique for each of us and so very magical!

The more I work with the Earth and the stars together with my own ancestral memories, both past and future, the more I realise that magic is inside each and every part of ourselves and this life. A phone in our pocket that allows us to see and speak to someone on the other side of the world would have seemed like magic to a person two hundred years ago. A vehicle moving us thousands of miles through the air would have been something of awe a thousand years ago. What we see as magical now may well, in another 50 years, be a normal daily occurrence. Or not! I suspect we will always have questions to which our answers take us into new territories with even more questions to ask. However, take small steps to expand the senses and watch how the abundance of this amazing and incredible existence opens up!

To begin a magical practice is to expand our senses and our connection with the planet and the Universe. Our ancestors would have used their senses of taste, hearing, touch, smell and sight far more than we do today and would have relied on those senses to keep safe and also for hunting food.

I'm intrigued by our senses and have been for a long time. We truly can grow them and expand just what we can sense. The extra- senses of, for example, clairaudience, clairsentience and clairvoyance are the expansion of our senses of hearing, feeling and seeing. I have suggestions for you to explore if you are curious to know more!

Please be mindful of where you are when trying anything new; by the way - keep safe ... just as our ancestors would have done!

1. **Taste**. When you next have a meal, really savour it. Even if you have prepared it from scratch, try to taste

the individual flavours. Can you identify the herbs and spices used? This is fun when out for a meal!

2. **Hearing**. Close your eyes and listen to the sounds around you. Really listen. And then extend your hearing to hear even more. What can you hear? And then ... what do you think you can hear?

3. **Touch**. Close your eyes and open your senses to what touches you. Can you feel the air, wind, and humidity touching your body? How does touching a flower feel? Or touching the fur of a pet? Describe it, and then describe it again!

4. **Smell.** Again, with eyes closed. What can you smell around you? Does the air have a scent? Can you smell flowers or scented oils? Do you like lavender or rose? What scents please you? Which do you dislike? Do any scents warn you of danger?

5. **Sight** - This is best suited for outdoors as I want you to look at a tree. Really look. See how the tree is made. The shape of the trunk, the branches, the leaves, the bark. Or another object. A stone. Draw it. Describe it. Half close your eyes and look at it. Draw it again. Is there an aura around it? Keep a note of this as, when we return to auras later in the year, you might like to go back to this one!

notes from the ancestors

Imagine for a moment our ancestors in their communities sheltering from the harsh Winter long nights: the cold and the dark. Limited supplies and those are dwindling by the day, keeping a fire alight for warmth and knowing that there would be no new crops for many months to come.

And then ... the shortest day of all and the longest night. Enough! Go outside and bang the drum. Make noise and wear the brightest of colours. Ask ... no ... TELL ... the Sun to return!

The dawning of a day where there was just that smallest amount more of daylight. The Sun appears above the horizon and is beginning to bring warmth. And maybe, just maybe, there might be crops growing in the fields this year.

And the opposite of what is happening on the other side of Earth.

Now, we will time-shift and move through the year to a moment where, suddenly, half a year has passed, and it's Summer Solstice. The longest day and the Sun is high in the sky. The point in our seasonal calendar when we feel less heat and see less daylight - the nights lengthen to encourage us into retreat.

And the opposite of what is happening on the other side of Earth.

Balance.

Our World is perfectly in balance with the seasons of the year. The clues from our universe are all there - when one part of the world is light, the other is dark. The Sun is high in the sky at noon somewhere right now - all are aligned and balanced. Our Earth, Gaia, is perfectly able to balance and refresh herself when left alone. Look at how Nature will fill gaps. Go to an abandoned railway track and see the flowers, wildlife and uninhibited growth that takes place. Then, watch it through the seasons ...

The seasonal cycle has been used for aeons to give a sense to agriculture of time to sow, nurture, harvest and use. And, if we are in tune with it, we can expand those energies to create a happier planet for ourselves and our grandchildren and theirs!

As we walk (or dance!) through the year by immersing ourselves into each season, there is a pulse as we join with nature and live the cycles - listen to the heartbeat.

Watch how, at similar times in the year, different cultures, different traditions, whatever tradition you look at, will have festivals. And yet they're celebrated in similar ways and with something at the root - by looking at different perspectives, we understand more. There may be a reason why these festivals are staggered. Perhaps there's something more going on with these festivals, being one festival one day, another festival the next day, another festival another day - a rhythm or a flow of joy and celebration sweeping the globe.

Rather than it being divisive (this belongs to that religion or to that tradition), perhaps we should be seeing the celebrations as a whole. And it's all a rhythm, and it's all a cycle.

What about the strength that is gathered as different groups of people celebrate similarly with a similar essence? And the energy of so many people, for so many thousands of years, watching the cycle of the sun moving through the signs of the zodiac.

Our Ancestors knew it was essential to understand where the Sun and the Moon were to plan for growing crops, harvesting and resting the soil. To really understand how the agricultural year works, how the seasons work and how the days unfold as a global responsibility towards keeping everyone fed and watered.

And so we have different religions, different traditions, different ways of celebrating the turn of the year, and they all have purpose to keep us in a flow of energy.

Do you have hope?

Hope in your heart that our planet Earth holds all that we, you and I, need to lead a wonderful, balanced life.

being

The Oak King and the Holly King doing battle is one of the most evocative illustrations of a myth being woven around something intrinsic to life itself. That we want the Sun to return with longer days of light and warmth still resonates when faced with the cold, the damp and long periods of darkness.

Could you write your own story of the two Kings battling to reign supreme for half a year?

This is an excellent time of the year to talk to family about what they remember of your ancestors. Bring your history to life by speaking family names and, if you have no idea who they were, create stories of how YOU would have lived in other times.

Some of my own biggest insights have come when I've sat quietly (usually, for me, in a stone circle or place with ancient history) and taken my awareness inside to talk to the landscape.

A favourite place of mine to visit is Castle Acre in North Norfolk (I love so many ancient sites and places but chose this one for this section), and as we walk up the hill, the history seems as if it is buzzing and fizzing all around. It is one of those places that calls out to the soul with conversations that have occurred over a thousand years or more. And it's where I had my first real experience of tuning into the people who had lived there before.

It was a sunny day, and the air was very still. Even though the green fields were busy with people milling around, there was a quietness that often occurs at places with ancient history. Sitting on the ground and on top of the hill meant the landscape stretched out in all directions.

And I closed my eyes to feel into that stretch.

The stretch of awareness in all directions of the compass. North, South, East and West. And then down through the earth to the centre of our planet to sense our Earth's solid nature and rock. I sat with that connection for a while ... would you like to join me in this? If so, go somewhere with history and stones half buried in the ground. Make sure you feel comfortable and safe closing your eyes, as this is easier for using the inner senses. And stretch that awareness through all of the compass directions and then downwards.

The last direction to be conscious of is upwards. As we zoom our awareness up through the clouds, sky, stars, and darkness, there will be our connection formed with infinity.

Now, we use our inner senses of sight, smell,
hearing and maybe even taste.

For a moment, focus through each sense with your mind...

What is beyond the physical world we know is still around us?

Can we picture a building newly created from stone with an entrance and a fire burning inside? Who is there, and how are they dressed? Is this an ancestral memory you've touched on?

I mentioned my insights at Castle Acre. My ancestors (maternal) were all from that area, and so I'm able to touch in with their lives in this way.

Remember that this is Winter, though (if you're reading this during Yule!), so I suggest keeping yourself warm. Our bodies can quickly drop in temperature when still.

Can you do this indoors and still connect with the landscape and the ancestors?

ABSOLUTELY!!

And it is even more life-affirming to ask the ancestors how they survived, laughed, celebrated, and danced at this time!

Sit quietly and connect in with the directions as discussed above. And then picture a barn or stone building with snow all around it. Who is inside? Are they surrounded by other people and animals or on their own? How are they using colour and music to bring the Sun back?

Record what you find. Repeat as many times as you want to and are able to. It's a great system to use at different times of the year to connect with the landscape. In another chapter, we'll talk about other ways of using the landscape to tune in to our natural frequencies; however, for now, and as it is our Yuletide 'Being' section - record by voice or word any fragments you remember!

doing

December through January is when the soil is resting, and the seeds beneath it are getting ready to grow. It's a time in our gardens to clear old growth away if we can whilst acknowledging that what is under the surface needs protection from the cold. Keeping paths clear of snow and ice for us and our four-legged families may be enough for us just now.

The colourful baubles and lights that have decorated our homes are special. At some point during January, you will undoubtedly be putting your decorations away until the next festive season. And this is when we can create some real magic! Wrap each ornament with care and thank it for helping your celebrations. Write a note to be read when the decorations are unwrapped of your intentions for the months ahead - just general, not too many details, as we will be doing more on this in our next season! But, for now, wish your future self good food, wonderful company and a Summer filled with laughter.

Remember the birds and wildlife, though, at this time. Put water out for them (yes, even in snow) and food. And watch, always watch, what is happening around us outdoors and inside.

Our garden has a stream at the bottom, and the water can get quite high at this time of the year. I've noticed that the moles move their tunnels further up the garden as the soil at the bottom of the garden becomes more waterlogged. The mole hills move to higher ground, and walking around the garden becomes interesting as it's apparent the tunnels are closer to the surface! But they're a part of the natural ecosystem of moving earth around and aerating the soil, so "thank you, moles" for helping us with the soil and preparing it for great growth in the coming year!

Make a plan for growing flowers and vegetables - even a window box or patio can be productive with thoughtful planting! Browse the seed catalogues and garden centre sites to build a picture of what you'd like to plant and when.

I know we laugh about making New Year's resolutions on January 1st, and by January 2nd, we've broken them. But, rather than on one date, this is a great overall time to think about what we want in the year ahead. And to mull over planting crops by looking in those seed catalogues.

What are you planting?

What do you want to blossom and bloom throughout the growing part of the year? This is the time to think about growth and where it will happen.

Or to dream of times to come when we can all sit outside and admire our spaces!

With that in mind, does the 'no dig' idea appeal? Take a look outside or at your garden plan, and decide whether you have space to try this this year.

Could you prepare a flower/vegetable bed or tub by just spreading a layer of compost on top? That's it, you know.... nothing more to do until planting time! The magic is happening under the surface, with the ecosystem leaping into action and the worms taking the new nutrients and mixing with the rotted matter already deep underground!

Research 'no dig' and also, while you're pondering on ecosystems and the sustainability of our gardens, begin to look at the slow-growing textile movements. More about that later in the book, when I'll share more about my flax growing, harvesting and weaving experiences, but in the interests of providing a beautiful home for those who will live after us, sustainability is key.

What could be more evocative of the Sun than sunflowers and the way they turn their flowers towards the Sun? And January is just the time to begin planting them.

Firstly, though, talk to your seeds. This is not as strange as it sounds. Each and every seed has all that it needs inside to evolve and grow into a plant. It has nutrients, moisture and the structure in place to become purpose. And each seed decides whether to grow and how. Nature is our greatest teacher always, and so, whilst we expect seeds to grow, we can never order plants to naturally behave in the way we want them to!

Prepare the pot you're using to grow the seeds with care. Is it a clean pot? Will there be drainage? Add the best compost you can manage and break it up with your hands if it's clumpy. You're creating the most optimum conditions for the plant to decide to grow in.

Hold the seeds you're about to plant in your hands and talk to them. What will each one be? Thank them for the journey they are about to take. Bless them with love and gently push them into the pot. Give them some water and then place them on a windowsill or somewhere light and just warm.

You'll keep them indoors until the frosts have subsided and the first green shoots begin to appear.

playing

This is where we find our celebrations and make some intentions clear to the Universe!

How will you shout out to the universe that things need to change? Would you make music and light a candle?

Music - learn a new instrument or make your own! There are people to help make your own drums, such as the Irish Bodhran or Indian Tabla. You can go on retreats and workshops for this or make your own. We will talk of music a lot in this book, so be guided over the next months towards what to make or learn. From penny whistles to tambourines, we have so much available to bring music to our homes.

Organise your own feast with a table groaning with food. Choose a table suitable in size - a coffee table is perfect if there's just you (and a cat or dog, of course!). Set the table with one extra place to allow for the expansion of family and friends ahead. And then choose food with purpose. A piece of fruit for abundance. A main course with spice for warmth and liveliness ahead. A drink to cheer and enjoy. And remember food for your animal friends - their favourite to let them know you will always look after them.

Dress for the occasion and take time - this is your party! And remember that, not so many generations ago, this conscious preparation and the 'theatre' around the main evening meal had a purpose. With stories to be told and songs sung after eating, the meal could take a whole evening.

Make sure that bright colours and lights surround you! Our intention is to send joyousness out for the Sun to return, bringing light, warmth and love.

Enjoy!

stillness

Our time of stillness for December and January is to recognise that, although nothing appears to be happening, the earth IS making preparations for Spring. Nothing ever stops or ends in this cycle of life all around us.

Do we take more than we give to our Planet?

This is when we give back energetically, and so I invite you:

To sit in complete silence. In natural light. Wear warm clothes so heating is at its lowest use of energy. Other than breathing and existing as matter in the space you are occupying, you are having no impact on the Earth at this precise moment. Take as long with this as is comfortable for you - nature is our teacher and, often, during this exercise, will give us a nudge of when to 'wake'.

Light a candle in a holder or turn on a light. Allow the light to gently bring you to the next step of consciousness. Slowly ease yourself into your world again.

Keep colour around you and the positive thoughts of warmer weather to come.

Whether this is for one minute, five or thirty, by giving the Earth time for rest and restoration, you HAVE made a difference!

Congratulations

dear friend

Dear Friend

In the season of Yule, we have begun our ways of welcoming the Sun-light back into our lives and to think about the year, the new year, ahead. The New Year is not determined by a calendar date, nor is it even determined by us in any way; it will be organised for us by the way the seasons develop.

Scotland celebrates one of the most famous poets in the world towards the end of January, usually on the 25th, with a Burns Night feast. Robert Burns was born in the 18th Century and gave us so much poetry that lives on and is spoken today. The words of Auld Lang Syne are sung at New Year and, possibly, is one of the most well-known songs for celebrating life and friendship. At this time of the year, with dark and cold evenings, what could be more confronting than to sit by a fire and read poetry ...

I am by your side throughout this book as you walk the eight seasons in your own way. Before we move gracefully into the next turn of the wheel of the year, I invite you to flick back through the pages of Yule and note which ideas, thoughts, stories, practises and celebrations you loved. Did you enjoy making up a new tale of Oak King and Holly King? Were you able to find a moment of stillness or explore your extra senses? How did your feast go? Are you expanding light by using colour and ringing bells?

There will be plenty of moments throughout the seasons to define what will bring you more joy as you walk forward, but for now, allow yourself the bliss of celebrating what Winter Solstice and the season of Yule brought to you!

As always, with love from Alison x

little spring

Winter Solstice /
Yule

Halloween/
Samhain

Imbolc

Autumn Equinox /
Harvest

Spring Equinox /
Ostara

Lammas /
Harvest

Beltane /
May Day

Summer Solstice /
Midsummer

little spring - february & march

This is a book like no other, just as your pathway through life is like that of no other. In walking the landscape of seasons, we are recognising the undulating hills and valleys of the different rhythms of the year. And each season is different. Every new season has subtle changes in energy, weather, power and intention and is punctuated by the eight solar days of celebration. Winter Solstice leads us into the season of Yule; Imbolc into the season of Little Spring; Spring Equinox into Spring; May Day into Little Summer; Summer Solstice into Summer; Lammas into First Harvest; Autumn Equinox into Harvest Festival time; Samhain into Winter; and then the cycle begins again but never exactly the same.

Nature is ever changing as she weaves her magic season by season. And so we have potentials to use the energy of change, rest, growth and integration in order to evolve and align ourselves.

Our season of Little Spring begins with the festival of Imbolc at the beginning of February. In the Wheel of the Year, this festival is between Winter Solstice and Spring Equinox and is known as one of the four cross-quarters. And it represents a huge pivot time for our outside world, with nature beginning to show us that she is waking up! Astrologically, Imbolc falls when the Sun reaches the mid-point between the Winter Solstice and Spring Equinox, often around 15º of Aquarius and during the first few days of February. In reality, this festival would have been celebrated at a time that suited a village or town and when the first green shoots appeared in the ground.

In the last chapter, we talked a lot about 'hope', especially for the Sun to return, bringing warmth and growth. Now, we begin the serious business of welcoming Spring with every sign of new growth appearing. Indeed, Imbolc is sometimes called THE festival of HOPE! There is a sense of being able to be outside for longer moments to not only watch nature but to begin to see where changes have occurred over the winter months. To begin the process of connecting with the outside world again and seeing the renewal of the power of the Sun.

Imagine the sense of freedom beckoning you outside for the first time in many weeks and then to see what might meet your gaze. Have walls and buildings held up through the cold months? Although there is still the quietness and the cold to keep us more indoors than out - it's as if nature were gently encouraging us out into the world again in tiny baby steps.

Both physically & spiritually, this season recognises the bridge between the cold & dark and the warm & light. The ground becomes softer through February and into March, and we can begin to plant seeds but very carefully. Not all of the frosts are over, and we still cannot plan to do much outside. But the tendrils of plants are beginning to show themselves, and so, too, are our dreams for the coming year.

I like to think of my dear friend and mentor Joyce Collin-Smith at this time ... well I think of her a lot, especially at the beginning of Spring. She loved this time with the snowdrops appearing, and it was always significant for her to hold some form of a celebration as soon as they appeared in her garden. Joyce started me on my spiritual journey more than anyone else did - or maybe she reawakened the memories inside me from my lineage that needed to appear in this particular lifetime. She was, and is, a very special person in my life, and I suspect you have one or two of those too.

There is a saying that:

> *"When the student is ready, the teacher will appear. When the student is truly ready... The teacher will disappear."*
> — *Tao Te Ching.*

And I was very much ready for a teacher and to connect with someone who cared. I was alone, broken and going through the daily motions of work, home, empty life. But I'd always wanted to learn the Tarot, and somehow, I saw a card in a newsagents advertising a six-week Tarot course held by Joyce in her home.

It was quite a journey for me to take at the time, as it was every Wednesday evening out in the depths of North Norfolk, and I didn't have a car! But I went and learnt and absorbed and loved the language of symbolism that the images of Tarot unlocked.

Joyce and I began a deep friendship, and she became family to me. She was also an extremely highly thought of and experienced astrologer, so it was a natural progression for me to continue studying and expanding my own knowledge into the esoteric.

A path that continues for me to this day, with now, nature as my greatest teacher.

Within a few weeks of that original six-week course, Joyce had booked a table at a Mind, Body & Spirit fair for us to share, giving readings for people. And that began my professional life in astrology, Tarot and symbolism. As fast as that! It all made so much sense, and that is what I truly hope for you, too … the sense part, I mean! You will find your own way along this amazing pathway of life, and if I can show some light bulb moments along the way, I will have completed my mission.

However, I have digressed, and you will have your own tale of what led you to this place of walking in rhythm with the earth.

Before we begin to explore more of this season, please take a moment to BE

grounding & connecting

Will you be able to do this outside for the first time this year? Or perhaps you've been regularly connecting with the landscape. It is the one thing I prioritise for myself and those I'm working with to make that connection with the ground and the Universe. In this way, we are ensuring that our inner radio dials are tuned in to our own unique frequencies and that our relationship with Earth within the Universe is maintained.

And it grounds us ... of course. Brings in an awareness of our sense of self.

Take a moment right now to sense where you are by standing or sitting still. There is no need to close your eyes or schedule this in your diary - just take a moment to reach your awareness down to the ground beneath your feet.

Plant yourself on the earth and, if you feel inclined, stamp your feet gently to remind your body where you are.

Connected to the Earth.

And then expand this moment by reminding yourself of the sky above your head and how the universe stretches out to infinity.

Connected to the Earth and the Universe.

You are tuning into the Earth and the Universe. It really is as simple as this. Use the moment to be aware of the Earth beneath your feet and the sky above your head. Feel the horizon of our planet stretching out from either side of you and in front and behind. And now you are grounded and tuned in to your own connected frequency of the Universe itself - magical!!

imbolc

The seeds find bravery

•••

This festival is sometimes called the Festival of Hope and also the Festival of Snowdrops. In the pagan calendar, children are given small gifts at this time to say welcome to the new energy beginning - or maybe well done for making it through the closeted winter months!

The tiny white snowdrop is often the first new flower that we see at this time of the year. For that reason, the Victorians gave the gentle snowdrop the importance of symbolising 'renewal' in their language of flowers. When creating posies, a snowdrop would indicate hope, renewal (of vows perhaps), trust that all would be well and joy ahead. Primroses also translate into 'new little one' and appear as Spring unfolds together with pansies and their words of love.

Newly born lambs are welcomed into the world, and the word "Imbolc" has roots in the phrase "lamb's milk".

In mythological terms, we welcome the Goddess waking to warm the earth ready for the inspiration of an abundance of growth. Mother Nature becomes the maiden of Spring. In practical terms, we have things to do:

Spring cleaning - After the harshness of cold winter days and nights, it's a welcome feeling to throw a window open and send fresh air through the house. There's an element of purity, or cleansing, of the earth to watch as the snows recede. And, thinking about our dwindling supplies, by cleaning and clearing, maybe we can find extra preserved food at a timely moment for this in-between time of old stores and before new crops appear.

Blessing the candles - This is a wonderful thanking of the candles for lighting our way through the dark months and also for giving light as we move forward. I have a beautiful candlelight reflection for you at the end of this chapter!

venus

The Romans dedicated this time to Venus as the goddess protector of vegetation and gardens: Venus - the goddess of beauty and abundance.

Astrologically, Venus rules the signs of both Taurus and Libra, so this allegiance with February actually does make sense. The Sun is in Taurus between April/ May and in Libra in September/ October, so it rules the times of the year for growth and harvest. And what could be better at this time of the year than celebrating and invoking a goddess of powerful growth and for a bountiful harvest! Especially for the Romans, who, quite clearly, needed to plant crops all along their pathway of dominating various countries. Later, we will look at the overlap, as always occurs, of festivals. Still, we can rest assured that the Roman celebration of Venus would have aligned with how other people and other cultures were also honouring the time of year.

The more I work with the planet Venus and where she appears in birth charts, the more I'm inclined towards her connections with earth magic. In the Tarot deck, Venus equates to The Empress card, and this also fits. The Empress with her flowing gowns and the fruits of harvest shown around her throne. She has the appearance of kindness and warmth, of caring and gentleness, and yet there is a ruthlessness for survival, too. The Empress energy is strongly powerful to urge all to be the best and achieve the most possible - to live out potential.

Venus energy gives permission for joy and beauty to flow. Remember that beauty is in the eye of the beholder and is different for each of us. In the growing of flax for the fibres to make textiles, we see pretty flowers as the plants grow. Yet nettle fibres are also of use for fabric and very strong, soft and sturdy for weaving when collected, dried and treated correctly. Pretty flowered flax and nettles that sting - both have fibres for weaving into practical garments and items!

Here is a key for this time of year.

The flow of life is beginning to be seen and felt.

Life always flows, of course, but seems slower in the dark months, and now, with the breathe of Spring growth appearing, is moving again in all expressions.

festivals & 'ho' to the sun

There are so many festivals at this time of the year, and I'm sure you will find many more than I have highlighted here. Isn't it just so fascinating that the whole world gathers its energy together at certain times in a wave of good intention - that's real, earth-based magic at work.

Chinese New Year is determined by the lunar cycle and will be, usually, the second new moon after Winter Solstice. The celebrations last around 15 days and take place from the end of January and into February.

A North American tradition has us observing the antics of the groundhog. If a groundhog emerges from his den at the beginning of February and sees his shadow, Winter will continue longer. No shadow heralds warmer weather coming, and so Groundhog Day has a rightful place in our list of festivals to welcome the returning Sun and warmth for growth!

As we move through February, the festivals continue! Shall we talk briefly about St. Valentine? There are many myths around St. Valentine. Was he the priest who secretly married couples to spare men from going to war? Or was he a rake who loved many women? Whoever he was and whatever his humble (or not!) beginnings, he has become the patron saint of love and represents opportunities galore to celebrate all things heart-based and love-orientated. Interestingly, he is also the Patron saint of beekeepers, which seems very fitting with honey being so sweet and the hives with their Queen bee in residence ... I feel we have quite a link here with Venus again.

Search around for festivals at this time, and you will find many to welcome abundance. From the dressing of wells to sending cards with pressed flowers (another tradition begun by the Victorians), the abundance of nature and the need for the warmth of love will never be far away.

And finally, for us walking the rhythm, we give a thought to Pancake Day or, rather, Shrove Tuesday. And we need to watch the lunar cycle again for the date. Easter Sunday is determined by the first full moon after the March Equinox (more about this in the next chapter!). Lent ends three days before Easter Sunday and will have lasted 40 days (excluding Sundays). By working backwards, Ash Wednesday is placed within the calendar and the time of sober preparation for what is to come within the Christian calendar. Shrove Tuesday is the eve of Ash Wednesday and the time, traditionally, to use up anything sweet and decadent before the thoughtful time of Lent ensues. Pancakes. Flour and butter and sugar and honey and ...

All of these festivals have echoes of the same stories at their heart, and there is one, just the one, real philosophy at work through them all ...

Hope as the Sun is returning for warmer, safer, well-fed times ahead.

bravery

What happens to our gentle seeds as they push up through the earth and out into the world? They have been resting in the warmth underground with all of the nutrients needed to grow when the time is right.

And the time is now.

Spring is beginning, and green shoots will appear above ground.

> *Something deep inside causes a shift to happen,*
> *and our seeds begin to realise they have the*
> *potential to be so much more.*

How brave of that seedling! They are about to grow above the edge of the ground and, for the first time, experience the light and moisture above. They don't know what the world will be like as they emerge from the comfortable earth.

Maybe flower beds have been altered.
Is it raining or dry?
Is it safe to sprout?

There may be something above ground that will immediately eat our green seedling or even a flock of birds that will demolish a whole field of new crops. There might be a new concrete structure in place or a tarmac road, which gives the puzzle of where our new plant will be able to find sunlight.

Our seedlings will show the ultimate bravery as they begin their journey towards becoming a flower, a plant, a fruit, etc. And Little Spring, beginning with Imbolc, prompts the very first seeds from deep underground to make that epic journey to above ground.

What happens when you are curious enough to
want to see what is beyond?

To let your dreams rise above?

notes from the ancestors

My Grandad Ted was brave. He didn't go to war. In fact, there were two world wars that occurred during his lifetime. He was of an age to go to war and to fight for his country in WW2. Any man who reached the age of 18 during the conflict was expected to sign up, and many who were younger actually found ways of doing so. To fight for one's country was the badge of honour expected.

It was an enormous sadness for my Grandad that he couldn't. He wasn't allowed to sign up due to his being deaf in one ear - a disability unseen by others. I have no idea if he was ever given a white feather, although, as he led a strange life during the war years and, particularly, the Second World War, he may not have been. However, he was aged between 7 and 11 during the First World War and, so, would have been well aware of what people thought of those who didn't fight. The white feather was given to those who were seen as cowards - men who didn't go to war. And it is documented that people were quite awful if someone wasn't seen to be 'doing their bit'.

What is 'doing their bit'? Is it being seen to be working more than others? Working harder or doing a job no one else wants to do? The term 'when we get the bit between our teeth' reflects that we are determined to achieve something. Something bitter tastes sour in the mouth, and, indeed, if we have a bitter taste in our mouths, it can be that a 'thing' is unsavoury or unpalatable. This 'bit' thing is interesting and seems to be used in different ways, although always with a tinge of toughness and work about it.

My Grandad Ted was a nurse. In fact, I have to expand on that as he was a male nurse in a time when men became doctors and women nurses. He didn't come from a monied background to train as a doctor but was driven to care. And care he did. He was a male nurse in a hospital for those with severe mental illnesses. I've called it 'severe mental illness'; however, in the early to mid-20th century, the men and women looked after behind the fences and locked doors of these institutions would have suffered from a wide range of problems.

Grandad was so proud of the fact that, during the war, they grew vegetables, kept animals and were completely self-sufficient. Remember I said he led a strange life during those war years? Imagine a hospital keeping people inside who couldn't be outside for their, and that of others, safety. Few staff remained as those who could, of course, went to war. Grandad Ted nursed and farmed inside the walls of an impenetrable area of gardens and locked buildings. He cared and, because I knew the man he was, lightened the spirits of everyone around him.

He was married with a young daughter, my mother, at the time.
He married my Nan in 1930, and my mother was born in 1931.
They only had one child, and, I suspect, the war put paid to any
plans to expand their family. Grandad and my Nan lived in
a cottage just outside the hospital walls. It was a small village
for those who worked in the hospital, and the homes were
known as hospital cottages. There were long lines of terraced
houses with small backyards and a community all around who
understood what went on behind the high walls dominating the
skyline.

My Nan read the tea leaves, and people, women mainly, would
come from miles around to hear her take on their questions.
My Grandad called it foolishness and would have nothing to do
with it. He was down to earth and a very practical man. Mind
you, so was Nan. She baked and made jams and jellies from
foraged fruit. Together they understood earth magic without
calling it that!

However, a day for Grandad Ted was a long one. His nursing
shifts were lengthy, and when he finished, the land work began
both on the hospital grounds and in his own backyard. He
didn't do things by half, and yet he would have said, if he'd ever
put it into words, he was just getting on with it because 'that's
what you do'. Get on with it. Do your bit. Don't speak about the
things that need to remain hidden. Turn the earth to provide
food. Care for those who cannot look after themselves. Grow
things. And live life.

And he saved money. On his retirement, they moved into a beautiful bungalow in the next village with a large garden and an outlook of fields. Oh my gosh, how he loved that garden. And how hard it must have been to save the money to buy a home outright with no mortgage at that time.

My Grandad Ted was brave. He did the things no one else spoke about, was very highly thought of in the world around him and brought cheer to those around. And he taught me the ways of the moon for gardening and much more.

He cared and grew things. And he whistled. And this is him with me!

being

I continue to work, holding workshops and giving readings for,
now, thousands of people from all over the world in both Tarot
and Astrology.   And I keep to the path I began while foraging
with Grandad Ted.

***There will be more of my story later in the book, but for
now, what about yours?***

You will have your own tale to tell of what led you to this place
of walking in rhythm with the earth. And others will enjoy
hearing it and adding their own. Whether you write it down,
tell it around a campfire or ponder on it - it is your story to tell.

Throughout the years, Storytellers have kept people in touch
with current affairs and history. There was only the spoken word
before newspapers and our rolling news channels took over.

The Fool in the Tarot deck represents the court jester and had the task of relaying news as he travelled the land. Think back to the times when courts, towns and villages would only have known what was happening outside their corner of the world by hearing from those who travelled. If you have a Tarot deck, take another look at the Fool. He will often have a dog at his feet shouting a warning as our Fool, sometimes, goes too close to the edge of a precipice. But he's not worried. He will step away and move onwards at the right moment. He also carries everything he needs inside the small bag he has on his shoulder.

He is like our seed! The Fool has everything he needs and travels 'out there', not knowing what he will come across. Our Fool has a mission, and that is to spread knowledge ... and laughter!

Take time to explore your story and then, perhaps, continue your journey into the lives of your ancestors.

Radio, TV and the internet have evolved the role of Soap operas to take over the telling of our day-to-day stories from that of our Fool. Dramatised tales of ordinary, or not so ordinary, folk living their lives with experiences we either associate with or not. How they cope, what they do, and when they make changes often keep us on the edge of our seats at times and hold our interest for many reasons.

You are the glorious star of the show and have your own story to tell!

And our ancestors are so worthy of a mention every now and again. By speaking their names and telling their stories, we not only remind ourselves of our place inside the ancestral line but also honour that they existed, loved and laughed and, of course, enabled us to!

doing

Once again, we can take our cues from nature to understand so much more of ourselves and each turn of the wheel of the year.

What will you plant in February? It will need to be behind glass, but what about the simple yet tasty cress? Cress seeds are inexpensive and grow quickly, so start some this week.

- Take an egg box and damp kitchen paper and sprinkle your seeds on top. Keep the paper damp and the box warmish.
- Or use small plant pots filled with compost and, again, behind glass. Keep watered.

And watch and observe. The second version, with our seeds beneath 'earth,' shows more of the bravery of the seeds, but whichever you decide on this month will give you your first crop of this year from this book! How special and magical, and remember to record your own insights as you watch that precious small plant weave its way upwards into life and to be the best it can be.

Walk outside when you can and connect to the earth. As you do, ponder on how Venus's energy shows herself to you. What do you find beautiful in the landscape around you? Is the world waking up and the ground beginning to have a slightly louder heartbeat?

See the snowdrops growing around trees where they can be assured of the warmer earth and shelter. But there can still be snow and ice at this time, too, and care is still needed to truly see the Winter out. Is the frost different after we've welcomed Imbolc? Just a thought for your notes ...

playing

This is the time to really begin to interact with nature, and, believe you me, as soon as we do that, nature responds!

The birds will be scouting for nests, and it's wonderful to watch them as they search out the best home for their new family. Some return to nests they use year after year, and others will find new ones.

They love natural fibres to build the inner sanctum where their precious eggs will be laid - can you offer anything? Allowing leaves and twigs to rest on the ground rather than sweep them up will help our birds in their build.

Nest boxes will benefit from a mini-clean out and a new layer of natural moss added - do this very early in February so that the birds know their nests will not be disturbed once chosen.

And keep things quiet around nests when you're aware of them. The rewards are amazing as our new bird families will emerge later in the year. It's a special moment to see the babies fledge and fly for the first time.

It's time to think about our inner language again and have some fun exploring it more. The word 'Scry' is taken from the Latin 'descry', which means to catch sight of or discover more about by looking very carefully. In our case, here we will be looking carefully by not focussing, so choose a place you feel safe to do this!

Take time to gently let your eyes go out of focus and let thoughts drift. Gazing into the embers of a fire will often bring unusual insights. Seeing the auras of trees (as we discussed in Yule) will show colours and, maybe, bring feelings into your awareness. We're playing in this part of the chapter, so let this exercise be a playful delve into your own language for a conversation with nature, which may be in another form of language to words.

Having conversations with nature, letting thoughts drift, 'seeing' into another dimension and even (as we will in a moment) just being still in our world all adds a depth to our wonderful experience of life.

stillness

Stillness is for listening and hearing the heartbeat of Gaia - our Earth. Stillness is for listening and hearing our own inner voice, our heartbeat. Stillness is also when we are completely silent and putting no stress on Earth whatsoever to give back to Earth by allowing time for her to recover.

I'm offering three ways to experience stillness at this time.

candle light time

This is a simple candle exercise that I've used for many years, and if you follow me or have been to one of my workshops, you may very well have done this before. Take a moment for the 'Stillness' part of Little Spring to do this and enjoy the space that is created for yourself. The process I've suggested below is just one of many different ways of using candle light for stillness, and the most important thing of all is that you enjoy this!

Are you ready to begin?

Gather together a candle, holder, lighter/matches, timer and maybe have your journal to hand, too!

This moment of stillness, and maybe also of visualisation, takes as long as you wish it to. Set a timer (or not!) for 5 minutes or half an hour - you decide, as this is when you connect with your heartbeat and also the heartbeat of the Earth.

1. Find a quiet, safe and peaceful place

2. Light the candle, place it in a holder, and gently watch the flame

3. Allow thoughts to gently move through your mind

4. If your attention wanders, that's fine ... just bring your attention back to the flame

5. Use my suggested words if you wish ... or just 'be.'

The light from the candle gently weaves
a pattern as the flame dances to its own music ...
Quietly opening intuition ...
Illumination gently showing what is possible
between earth and the sky above ...
The heart within the glow flickers and changes ...
Thank you for lighting the darkness!
Thank you for lighting the way ahead!
Thank you for showing the fragility and yet the strength of life!
Thank you!

6. Extinguish the flame

7. Allow time to adjust to the world by writing or remembering what just happened.

quietly giving

Similar to last month, this is a wonderful practice to include each week in these months of our Earth restoring itself. Set an intention of giving moments of your time for the earth herself.

This will give our earth some respite from the stresses and strains we exert on her during our lives. Now, obviously, we are here to live our experience on earth and so need to be getting on with all that entails. However, just for moments, give back by allowing Earth to just be.

So prepare a beautiful, safe space with no distractions. Warm and comfortable. Natural light. And sit, or lay down wrapped in a blanket, and allow some moments to pass of 'nothingness'. There is always 'something'; however, encourage the 'nothing'.

And this is the easiest of all - by allowing our earth some moments to do whatever she wants so we also realign or reset ourselves!

the bravery of moving

And our third way of experiencing stillness is a visualisation. In this, we will move our attention between the above ground and the below ground. Once again, find a quiet, safe, peaceful and warm space and read the visualisation below a few times to familiarise yourself with it. Then, gently close your eyes and breathe normally while your inner self travels to the bridge.

A visualisation of moving between below and above ground.

Standing on a bridge
Looking at the water below
And then, deeper beneath the bed of the river and,
the earth blow
Slowly, your thoughts rise upwards through the earth and water
Up above the bridge and out into the air
You gaze up at the sky and are thankful
Full of thanks for the earth, the water, the sky and the fire of the
Sun

Thank you!

Allow time to adjust to the world by writing or remembering what just happened as you open your eyes and return to the here and now.

dear friend

Dear friend,

In the season of Little Spring, beginning at the Festival of
Imbolc, we continue to welcome the Sun, expanding our hours
of daylight. Newborn lambs, birds searching for nests, tiny
seedlings making their way above ground and yet sometimes
there is still snow and even ice. We are gently encouraged to
ponder on what is outside.

Before we move gracefully into the next turn of the wheel of the
year, I invite you to flick back through the pages of Imbolc and
note which ideas, thoughts, stories, practises and celebrations
resonated. Did you enjoy planting some cress? Were you inspired
to think about your own ancestors and the lives they led? Which,
if any, of the stillness practises helped you to find your own sense
of 'still' or perhaps you have your own?

There will be plenty of moments throughout the seasons to define
what will bring you more joy as you walk forward, but for now,

just allow yourself the bliss of celebrating what Imbolc and the season of Little Spring brought to you!

As always, with love from Alison x

spring

Winter Solstice /
Yule

Halloween/
Samhain

Imbolc

Autumn Equinox /
Harvest

Spring Equinox /
Ostara

Lammas /
Harvest

Beltane /
May Day

Summer Solstice /
Midsummer

spring - march & april

The Sun moves into the zodiac sign of Pisces around the 21st of February. Between the Festival of Imbolc and Spring Equinox of Pisces, the twelfth sign of the zodiac holds memories and contains a wisdom ready to take forward into the new cycle when the Sun moves out of Pisces and into Aries.

The moment of the Sun moving into Aries is our Spring Equinox with a balance of equal light and dark light. The Equinox plays an important role in what is happening for our new season of Spring, and we'll look at our time of equal-ness and equilibrium in a while. The turning point between Little Spring and Spring, the Equinox, is a major shift physically and spiritually.

Now, it is March, and we're moving through the month and on into April. The flowers are appearing more and more in our gardens and hedgerows. There is physical work required of us as the earth warms and our gardens need attention. Occasionally, there will still be snow, but never for long, and although the weather can be completely changeable, we can go outside much more with curiosity and wonder - the Northern realm of our planet is waking up with a vigour and an energy. The yellow daffodil plants bloom with golden trumpet flowers gazing up to the Sun.

Daffodils are interesting, well all of nature is, of course; however, the gentle daffodil is especially so! The yellow/white flower takes over from the gentle snowdrop of little Spring and becomes as abundant as possible. And there is a determination displayed of life from our pretty daffodils as they turn their flowers towards the sun for maximum light and lower their flowers when the weather is hard. And as they quickly recover as soon as the wind or rain stops, we have an early sign of how robust nature is!

The birds now begin family building in earnest, and we may just see a blur of wings as they go into and out of their nesting boxes or nests. There are so many stories, legends and tales to uncover for this time, but there is also a logic too. Eggs have been laid in the nests, and future families are created. The equinox moment is where we see an exact time of equal light and dark. Constellation-wise, the Sun moves into Aries - I'll possibly mention that again later in this chapter! The time of Spring in our Northern hemisphere begins when the Sun moves into the sign of Aries, as we've seen and then continues as the Sun moves into the zodiac sign of Taurus at around the 21st of April.

However, there is so much more to this time, and we need to consider the astrology for another layer of our understanding of just what is happening here—memories, both old and those about to be made. Our brave seedlings who have started their new life above the ground are now about to become aware of the truthfulness of being out in the open. As they break through the earth, they are exploring what is real and what is an illusion.

However, with all of the energy needed for this amazing push into Spring, we need to be aware of our own selves more than ever! And so we take time for our body, mind, spirit and soul to **BE**

grounding & connecting

The position that we hold on planet Earth belongs to us at the moment we occupy it. No one else has that same place on the Earth in this particular moment in time!

One or all of this may resonate ...

Do you have a regular practice of going outside, weather permitting, of course, and tuning your inner radio dial to the planet and the Universe?

Are you committing daily to re-establishing your connection with the Planet, your place on it and the universe?

Have you noticed a change in frequency? More awareness of your sense of self and your own strong position on earth?

Make an appointment with yourself to go outside at dawn one day this week. I really recommend the sheer magic of sunrise!

Sunrise with all of the golden potential of the day ahead.

Take a moment to sense where you are by standing (or sitting) still and reach your awareness down to the ground beneath your feet. You've made a date with yourself to do this, so perhaps, if you can, take a little longer than usual to do this.

Connect to the Earth.

And then expand your awareness out to the sky above your head and the infinity of the universe and space.

Connected to the Earth and the Universe.

Tuning your frequency into the Earth and the Universe.

Use the moment to be aware of the Earth beneath your feet and the sky above your head. Feel the horizon of our planet stretching out from either side of you and in front and behind. And now you are grounded and dialled into your own connected frequency of the Universe itself - magical!!

Watch a sunrise with all of the magical potential of the day ahead!

spring equinox

The festival of Spring Equinox is when we begin to see springtime take hold, and the equinox itself is determined by the Sun moving into the sign of Aries.

Aries, as the first sign of the new cycle of the zodiac, is ruled by planet Mars and gets the wheel of the agricultural year well and truly turning. In Medieval times, it signified a time when rents were due, and perhaps, we still see a nod to that with taxes often being calculated around this time.

I've already mentioned that there is equal light and dark at this time of Equinox, and after this moment, the days will become longer than nights. Work will start in fields, and we emerge out into the warmer weather when we can.

There may still be snow, and yet the melting snow offers moisture for the Earth. The Sun offers more and more heat daily, gently and not all at once, so to parch the ground before our seeds have had a chance to take root and grow.

Nature teaches us at every moment, and the strongest insights for us all are found inside her natural rhythm. The Spring Equinox represents balance, equal light and dark, alters our rhythms to expect longer days than nights and shifts the Northern Hemisphere into joyful growth and the satisfaction of having made it through a long Winter.

> *That's quite a lot to receive from one moment, and yet it is a crucial moment as our year unfolds.*

festivals & 'ho' to the sun

There are other festivals and ways of looking at calendars at this time, and all celebrate the warmth returning and new beginnings. One example, steeped in ancient history, is the use of the Persian calendar. Using lunar and solar cycles, the Persian New Year is celebrated at the Spring Equinox. Indeed, it is also celebrated as a new year in the Druid calendar.

Look out for celebrations, or even pageants, around this time, a distinctive 'New Year' feel to them!

A little more about the astrology of this particular festival and remember that at Spring Equinox, the Sun moves into the astrological sign of Aries. Well, Aries is ruled by the planet Mars, and that red planet offers fire energy and ignition. Indeed, Mars is THE planet for starting something and giving energy to an action or activity. Think of the starter motor in a car with the spark of the ignition key, and there is Mars energy.

This is the time to watch for signs of renewal or rebirth, and the Christian tradition of Easter also has a resonance in no small way with the older myths and stories based around this time.

Just for a moment, think of our Easter Eggs. Chocolate eggs are given on Easter Sunday as a symbol of being out of Lent and the resurrection of Jesus three days after the crucifixion. At the end of Lent, rich, sugary foods are allowed into the diet. And eggs ... why eggs?

egg

There is nothing more powerful than an egg for both the symbolism and the actual birth of a new life. The eggs within a woman, those of nesting birds - an egg brings life into being.

Looking back in village records, we find egg and spoon races for village fetes and, even further back, eggs being hidden for children to find at this time of the year. And that speaks volumes for the joy that obviously was being felt at an abundance of food beginning to appear!

The ancient Egyptians would paint eggs and give them as good luck charms.

It's a joyful time, and every part of stories from this time of the year reflects that.

Sometimes, you will see mention of the Spring Equinox called Ostara. Ostara was the Anglo-Saxon goddess of the dawn, and there's mythology in the ancient Germanic traditions of the goddess of fertility. We can also see a source of the word oestrogen from Ostara, especially when we consider the fertility of the female cycle.

If we go back into mythology and Celtic lore, we read of Ostara as the goddess who transformed a bird into a hare. The hares danced and laid colourful eggs as gifts for the goddess. A representation of the circle of life ... and the hare as a symbol for Ostara. It is still considered lucky to see hares dance!

The use of decorations could have gone into the 'Being, Doing, Playing and Stillness' part of the book; however, it seems to crossover all of those and so:

decorations

Eggs

Carefully boil an egg or two in water that has a natural dye added to it. Onion skins produce a light golden colour. Beetroot, a reddish purple. Nettles a pale green. Once cooled, the egg can be further painted, adorned with ribbons or flowers and displayed or used to hide for children to find, as I mentioned before!

Hats

The Easter bonnet also has such a history as the first time girls would have emerged out into the Spring warmth and wanted to look pretty. Wearing colourful ribbons and flowers in the hair would bring joy after the cold and dark months for all who saw!

Entrances and doorways

Use spring flowers to create posies and decorate the front doors of our homes. By bringing colour to the outside of our houses and buildings, we encourage new growth and even more abundance!

Colours

Yellow is the colour of the Sun and of light everywhere. White is another colour for Spring, and we also look at the springtime flowers for more hints.

Other symbols

The use of symbolism, a subject I return to time and again as it is at the fundamental root of all manifestation and celebration, is a potent way of bringing extra energy to our actions when there just are not enough words! And so, if you're working some magic at this time, there are some great items to use:

- Garlic and onions - to symbolise the planet Mars.
- Anything red will also bring in Mars energy.
- Daffodils, tulips & crocuses - symbolising spring getting stronger and crocuses are THE symbol for new life along with eggs.
- Eggs.
- A picture, or ornament, of a hare.

persephone & demeter

The tale of Persephone and her mother, Demeter, with its roots in Greek mythology, is so deeply entwined with our ancestral memories of the Spring and Autumn Equinoxes that we need to spend time with these two women as we muse on the season of Spring.

Remember the battle of the Oak King and the Holly King, which gives us our marker points of the Solstices and the times when our days or nights lengthen depending on who wins the battle for the crown?

Persephone and Demeter have a similar role to fulfil at the two equinoxes.

Demeter is, in mythology, the goddess of agriculture and abundance. And the consort of Zeus. Their daughter was Persephone, known throughout all the lands for her beauty, joy, and kindness of love.

And that lively and lovely nature of Persephone came to the attention of Hades, the lord of the underworld, who fell in love with her and wanted her for his own. Demeter refused to give her daughter to him and battled to keep her by her side. There was more at stake as Hades lived below ground, and if Persephone were to go to him, then she would disappear from the earth.

But Hades was determined and kidnapped her. Stories are different from this dark time; however, it is clear that he took her down through the labyrinth of paths and into his underworld realm.

Demeter, having anticipated that something like this may happen, gave Persephone a ball of golden string so that she would never lose her connection with her mother and all that was on earth. And Persephone took that ball of string and laid it out as she walked down into the underworld.

Now, there was a real battle of wills between Hades and Demeter, and eventually, they came to an agreement. They would share the lovely Persephone each for six months of the year.

And so Persephone used the golden thread to return to the surface of Earth, and, as she emerged, flowers bloomed and birds sang. Joyous nature became abundant, and the warmth returned. Mother and daughter reunited, and Spring turns into Summer.

The story of Demeter and Persephone is woven into our ancestral memories of Spring emerging from the cold depths of Winter and of growth after silence.

the labyrinth

Mazes and labyrinths have been used since ancient times. They're part of our landscape, and that can be our inner landscape as well as the outer.

I took part in making a labyrinth as part of the celebrations in Norwich for the Millennium. We created it on December 31st 1999, and it was just so beautiful, with the pathway marked by tea lights inside little glass jars. It was built in an afternoon and there for the evening, and it's actually permanent now in the crypt at Norwich Cathedral. It is an example of how people could all come together at that time and celebrate something very special at the turn of the century.

*Labyrinths differ from mazes as there is only
one way in and one way out.*

I've added a whole segment for you on drawing a labyrinth (step by step!) in the 'Playing' section, and it is a very magical practise. Drawing a labyrinth helps the mind focus in a different way to anything else I've discovered. Use it as a meditative tool or as a time for pondering and letting the mind drift whilst concentrating on the main thing of drawing the lines. We have one in our garden, five circuits, and I walk it to remember or access answers.

But it does require concentration, and whenever I've tried to film myself walking and talking, it inevitably goes wrong somewhere!

But something I've wanted to show you was how we built our labyrinth. And this is how we actually built it in our garden. We don't have enough space for a full seven-circuit labyrinth, so this is a five-circuit labyrinth. We drew it and then staked it out. And then we start to build it.

And so this is it in its early, very, very early stages!

And this is what greets us at the end as we emerge from walking the labyrinth!

notes from the ancestors

The Ways of the Moon.

My Grandad Ted taught me the ways of the moon. My childhood was very different to that of my brother. I was born first, and as my mother was more than 30 when she had me, my birth changed her life. At least, that's what I think. Now.

My mother, Polly, had a good life until me. She had a job as a receptionist for a large insurance company and loved it. Her cousin ran a very large, lively pub in the centre of Norwich, and Mum helped out behind the bar. It was in the pub that she met my Dad and, as she was age 30 and he was 5 years older, they married quickly - this is something I always loved as I suspect they swept each other off their feet!

Within a year of marrying, she had me, and they moved to a different county where the work was for my Dad. By the time I was six, they had moved back to Norfolk, and Mum was happier being back near her Mum and Dad. My brother was born in Norfolk, was a happy baby from the word go and represented moving back to a place my Mum loved.

During the school holidays, I used to look after my brother while Mum and Dad worked. And, when Mum took a holiday to spend time at home, I stayed with Nan and Grandad Ted. Those were such special times, hugely influential in my life, and I remember a bed with sheets, blankets, bolster and eiderdown. They lived in the countryside in a bungalow with gardens and fields all around. And stars. I remember the stars stretching out in the sky, looking like diamonds.

Grandad took me out walking along country lanes, picking fruit and conkers. He talked to me about the moon and how he would wish on a full moon for more of whatever his thoughts had turned to. And he would turn the coins over in his pocket on a new moon for more money to come in.

There's a lot of good in the world.

Looking back, I now know that he was working with the energies we call 'attraction', and yet, bearing in mind the sheer down-to-earth attitude he had towards life, he wouldn't have called it anything other than "that's what we do".

And he followed the cycles of the moon for gardening and growing vegetables, too. Again, we now call it bio-dynamic gardening, and there is a lot of information and scientific data proving the effectiveness of using the lunar cycles in this way. Grandad Ted just knew it worked and grew fruit and vegetables to feed his family and others.

Did I tell you about the skies? There is nothing quite like a Norfolk sky for drama and scale. Huge skies and a panorama of stars to take the breath away.

Grandad's birth has a mystery attached to it, not unusual for the time. He was born in 1907 in Hackney, London. When his mother, with baby Ted, returned to her family in North Norfolk, she became his Aunt, and his grandmother brought him up as her own. Nellie, his real Mum, had been working in a grand house as a maid and never spoke of who Ted's father was. She did marry later, but they never had any children.

So Grandad Ted was brought up in North Norfolk, where the skies would have been even more clear than we can possibly imagine now. His early years were spent in a small coastal town where everyone really did know their neighbours, and religion and superstition played a huge role in daily life. He was clever and studied enough to become the amazing nurse he later qualified as.

There are tales from the North Norfolk coast of smugglers and shipwrecks; tough winters and traditions based on the religious calendar; a school room with a map of the world on the wall; whispered 'news' supposedly from the big city of Norwich … London would have been too distant to even enter general conversation! No wonder Nellie was able to go to London to have her baby in secret!

The coastal town was a thriving fishing port, and seafarers of all description lived and worked there. The women waited on the docks for their men to come back from what could be treacherous seas.

Shipwrecks and smugglers, fishermen and dock workers, and traders of all descriptions had their place and their work to do. And the light from the Sun and the Moon was an intrinsic part of what could be done and when!

The dark of the moon, just before the new moon, was for deeds for which no light was required. Travel in secret during a dark moon if you were familiar with the terrain. And a Full Moon? A sky full of light lengthened the working day, and more could be accomplished.

Practical Moonlight.
Attraction moonlight.
A beautiful beaming moon in the sky.

My grandad instilled it all in me, and I appreciate his wisdom whenever I look at the moon!

being

This is where we immerse our deeper self into the mythology and nature for this time of the year - and so I have a choice of two ways of 'being' for you!

Demeter and Persephone.

The tale of Mother Nature watching growth disappear only to re-emerge at Spring. Although we will return to this in Autumn and the opposite Equinox, why not consider your own story of emerging from some part of your life and into a new one? As the Sun rises, a new day dawns, and there is the promise of love and laughter, growth and abundance, new people to meet and new adventures to begin.

Growing with the Moon.

Make a note of the cycle of the moon for the months of March and April.

When is the New Moon?

Will you set aside a time to plant a seed on the New Moon and nurture it with warmth and just enough water over the next two weeks?

When is the Full Moon?

Your seed may be showing itself by now ... or not! But it will be growing, and you can celebrate it, nurture it and yet, with the waning moon energy, perhaps be a little more gentle with it.

Whatever you plant may require several cycles of the moon in order to blossom and bloom into its full potential ...

doing

A pendulum is one of my favourite 'ways' to access that connection between intuition and our connection to the Divine source.

Dowsing

There are many pendulums available, and when looking for one, choose the one which you feel most comfortable with. There is something quite special about our connection with the crystal of a pendulum, and my recommendation would be for a clear quartz crystal, amethyst or rose quartz. Or you can use a pendant or even make your own, and very good results can come from suspending a wedding ring using thread. The important part of the exercise is that whatever is suspended is allowed to move freely.

Be still, align and ground. In order to do this, take any of the grounding and connecting exercises that begin each chapter.

Hold your pendulum lightly between thumb and forefinger, and from around shoulder height so that the crystal is about level with your heart or slightly below. When it stops spinning or moving and is still, ask it questions. These can be spoken out loud or inwardly - take your time over this part, though, as much like preparing a room for decorating, how well the connection is established will lead to clearer answers later on.

My name is (correct name)
My name is (incorrect name)

Continue by asking questions along the lines of where you live and then follow with something outrageous.

Note the way the pendulum swings. You are accessing the 'yes' and the 'no' that is already known deep inside of you by your intuition. It's not logical and, indeed, switches 'off' the logic brain!

And now you are ready to begin to dowse.

A great example of the use of this is when making up a flower remedy. Hold the pendulum over each one and ask, 'Is this what I need?' or 'Is this what X needs?'. Some people will use the pendulum for their choice of food or crystal. You may find it interesting to use the pendulum to help choose Tarot cards.

Spread the cards out and then hold the pendulum over them. Watch for the yes or no reaction.

Always begin each dowsing session with asking your true and false questions as the 'yes' and 'no' will often be different - remember that you're establishing a connection with your intuition, and that's a powerful tool!

The pendulum can be used in the same way as dowsing rods to divine for water or earth energies - it's all in the intention set at the beginning of each session with your pendulum.

I'm also going to add a 'pendulum disclaimer' here ... using ways and means of accessing the intuition can become quickly addictive, and that may lead to beginning to see answers as 'out there' or even repeating until we get the answer we want to hear rather than a clear, intuitive one. Our intuition is our inner language and so available to us all from within - using something such as a pendulum gives our intuition permission to speak and allows us to hear it! Go gently and become used to how this works! And enjoy!!

playing

Will you find a labyrinth to walk? Remember that a labyrinth is different to a maze, although mazes are fun to explore. Make an arrangement with yourself to go and find one this March/ April time and walk it purposefully and with intention. As you walk it, make sure to pause in the centre before turning to return to the beginning. The path is the same yet will, most likely, look very different from the perspective of 'the other way'.

And it can also be fun, insightful, addictive and interesting to draw your own labyrinth - I promised a 'step by step' and here it is ...

1. Begin with drawing an equal-armed cross in the centre of your page.

2. Draw the corners and then a dot in the centre of each corner.

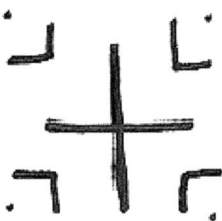

3. Make the first connecting line.

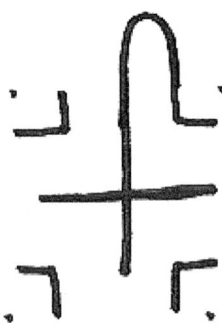

4. And the next connecting line.

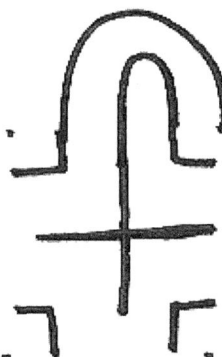

5. Now, it starts to become a little more complex (believe me when I say this can take a while!) And the next line.

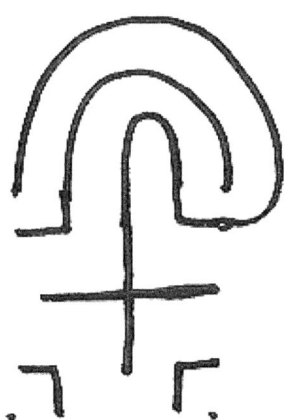

6. Time for another.

7. And another.

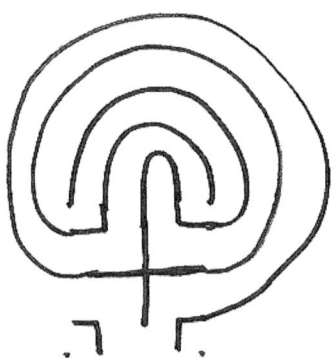

8. Not far now.

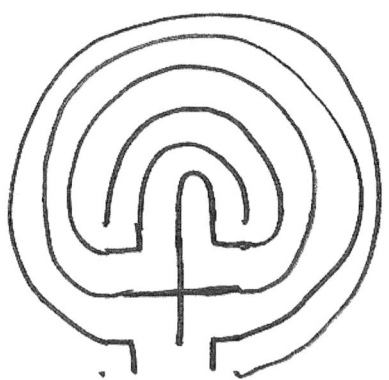

9. Almost completed, but not quite.

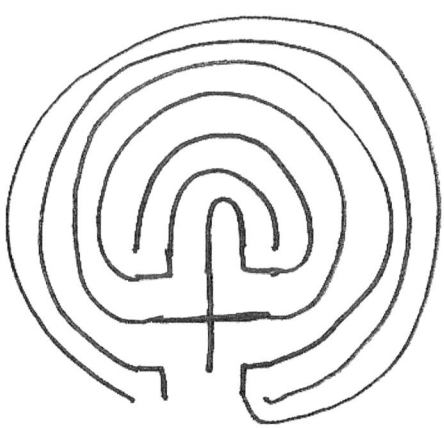

10. Completion.

Congratulations!

stillness

Use your labyrinth that you've drawn and sit with it. Trace the journey with your finger and keep your awareness of the movement. Let your imagination dwell on the space between the lines and concentrate on taking the path to the centre. Will you descend as you move along the path or ascend?

When you walk a labyrinth, use the experience to connect with the ground beneath your feet each step of the way. Listen to your heartbeat as you connect with that of the labyrinth. Walk forward towards the centre; there is only one way to go, and you cannot get lost. And then take a moment at the centre to be still and silent - just that. No expectations. A pure moment of stillness. Slowly turn and retrace your steps. As you emerge from the labyrinth, raise your face to the light and greet a new reality or perspective on life.

dear friend

Dear friend,

The Equinox brought balance for us with equal light and dark, and now, as it's Springtime, we're able to go out into the world and see growth happening all around.

Did you walk a labyrinth? Or draw one, perhaps? Maybe you made one out of stones on the seashore? This is a special connection we have now, you and I, of exploring the labyrinth together, and please give time for your own deliberations of emerging out into the sunlight, just as Demeter does, into a wonderful world above ground!

Before we move gracefully into the next turn of the wheel of the year, I invite you to flick back through the pages of this chapter and note which ideas, thoughts, stories, practises and celebrations resonated. Maybe you made a pretty bonnet or painted an egg or, and here is where I celebrate the uniqueness of you, perhaps you chose to just be in a moment of stillness and calm outside in nature!

There will be plenty of moments throughout the seasons to define what will bring you more joy as you walk forward, but for now, just allow yourself the bliss of celebrating what the Equinox and the season of Spring have brought to you and to those around you!

As always, with love from Alison x

little summer

Winter Solstice /
Yule

Halloween/
Samhain

Imbolc

Autumn Equinox /
Harvest

Spring Equinox /
Ostara

Lammas /
Harvest

Beltane /
May Day

Summer Solstice /
Midsummer

little summer - may & june

The festival of Beltane (around the first of May) is one of joyous celebration as we triumphantly begin to welcome Summer. The Sun is in the sign of Taurus and has a great deal to say about the connection between the material and spiritual ... as we shall see!

With maypole dancing, Queens and Kings, flowers and bounty - this is THE time to go outside, celebrate and dip into real life. There is an expansion of spiritual knowledge and understanding of lessons received from nature available of the deep transformations occurring.

Energetically, this time represents a big shift for our bodies, minds and spirits as the days lengthen and the planted seeds are growing. On a deeper level, our ancestral memories are waking as our yearning for more than the material begins. We've spent months living in the cold, wondering whether our supplies would last, and now it's off outside into the abundance that awaits from nature.

And so we continue our daily practice of grounding and connecting, which, now more than ever, takes some discipline to maintain in our morning routines each day. It will be easy to forget about our inner selves as we experience more and more of the outside world; however, a balance is required ...

And so my regular invitation to you is similar to last month and yet, as always, there is a change to recognise the season ...

grounding & connecting

The position that we hold on planet Earth belongs to us in the moment we occupy it. This is such a crucial part of our existence on planet Earth. No one else has that same place on the earth in this particular moment in time!

Think about it for a moment. Would even someone in the same building as you but on a higher floor have the same position in time and space? The coordinates may be the same, but, in actual fact, the perspective that you have on the world through your senses is uniquely YOURS.

This is a good opportunity to revisit the senses (we first started to consider them in Yule season), as they will be on high alert now as we go outside into the May/June air to talk and be social. Especially as we are beginning this new season with the Sun in Taurus and, in mid-May, the Sun will move into the very social sign of Gemini!

Take a moment to sense where you are by standing (or sitting) still and reach your awareness down to the ground beneath your feet.

Connect to the Earth.

And then expand your awareness out to the sky above your head and the infinity of the universe and space.

Connected to the Earth and the Universe.
Tuning your frequency into the Earth and the Universe.

What taste is in your mouth?

Take a moment to consider ...

What can you hear around you?

Take this time to listen to the sounds and then to listen some more ...

What touches you?

Is there a breeze, air, or humidity?

Can you reach out and touch something, whether grass, flooring, a tree, a table ...

What smells are there around?

Do you smell flowers and nature? Or maybe there are wafts of cooking ...

What do you see?

Look and look again. Describe what you see to yourself ...

Use the moment to be fully aware of the Earth beneath your feet and the sky above your head.

Take what you've learned from your senses to know more about 'where' you are.

And then feel the horizon of our planet stretching out from either side of you and in front and behind.

> **And now you are grounded and tuned in to your own connected frequency of the Universe itself - magical!!**

beltane

**The festival of the beginnings of Summer
and when two become three ...**

Beginning of May

Each of the festivals celebrates the turning wheel of the year
with the spirit of transformation as one season turns into
another. Beltane is, perhaps, one of the most deeply Magical
times as it is opposite the time of Samhain, or Halloween, in our
calendar of festivals. In personal astrology, it is so useful to look
at opposites - opposite houses, signs, planets. The saying about
opposites attract holds much for us to uncover when we think
about what is opposite 'us'. And so, as we reach the festival of
Beltane, it is worth also thinking about Samhain as when the
veil between worlds is at its thinnest, and we can walk between
realms if we so wish. There is much more, and we'll uncover
that when we get to that festival later in the year, but what does
'walking through invisible doors' offer us for Beltane?

In the study of alchemy, we wonder at the lengths true alchemists have gone in order to produce the metal of gold and then translate it into the symbolism of ourselves transforming to find our inner gold. This month of May, leading us into June, shows us through nature how seeds have become plants, eggs have hatched into birds, and the pollen from plants flies off to land who knows where.

Nature is transforming and evolving and growing
and being so very special!

The name Beltane seems to have come from terms meaning 'bright fire' or 'beautiful fire', and one thing is for sure: the concept of fire is important.

There are so many superstitions related to May Day and this festival. An interesting one is that it is bad luck to light a fire until after your neighbours have lit theirs.... now ... how would a fire ever get lit? There are traditions to appease the fairy folk and also those to ward them away. This is a time when animals are giving a lot of milk and crops are abundant. And so we give our neighbours bounty to say thank you, and yet ... there are also tales of not giving in case you are giving away power! I'm including all of this as a way of emphasising the element of balance at this time and of standing in our own power.

Spiritual and material.
Bounty for one and bounty for all.

Maybe the key here (and I'm so aware of the Sun being in the sign of Taurus moving into Gemini around the 21st of May) is that this is a time for recognising our own bounty and celebrating it, and then going out into the world to help others share theirs!

Maytime represents the first time our ancestors could really rely on being outside and to plan for joyous festivals. To celebrate life and land becoming truly abundant and green. Plants are blossoming, birds are singing, young birds and animals are being reared and, particularly, the hawthorn blossoms in the hedgerows. There is an old saying, 'cast n'er a clout until the May is out,' and interpretations of this can vary. It does have instructions for us to dress warmly, but whether until the Hawthorn, or May, is flowering or the month of May is ended - well, I'll leave it to you!

Interestingly, this is the only time that Hawthorne is allowed in the home as a decoration and for good luck. We celebrate that nature is looking pretty again with flowers showing us colour, and there's another old saying that 'a swarm of bees is worth much hay' and heralding even more bounty to come.

If you dream of Hawthorne, it's symbolising better days to come with creative abundance!

So let's think about where Beltane is in our Wheel of the Year and, not only opposite Samhain, it is also between those two astrological points of Spring Equinox and Summer Solstice.

Beltane is when the Sun is in the middle of the sign of Taurus and is usually celebrated around the first day of May. Due to the party atmosphere surrounding this festival, though, it would have been arranged for when people could get together for a day and an evening - so a decent amount of time needed to be set aside. A day of no work and no rain, perhaps! This is an outward festival, and it's a time of merriment.

The festival is a celebration of plenty, abundance and prettiness! It's the time for weddings, unions and also handfastings or weddings. The name of the month, May, can be traced back to the Roman goddess Maya, who was responsible for everything that blossomed and bloomed. Take a look at the Tarot card, the three of Cups, which, I feel, says everything about this time!

***And Spring has now transformed into the
first day of Summer ...***

the may queen chooses her king

A pretty girl and a handsome man are joined together to move through the streets in a procession and receive their crowns of flowers in order to create a child. This is a highly charged and symbolic action as it represents the goddess and god from ancient times coming together out in the open to create new life. The stories behind this myth are slightly different (as in all myths, they have evolved with age!); however, whichever way you look at this story, it is about two human beings meeting in order to create new life. The continuance of human life. Life force. To ensure lineage, abundance, fertility, and good crops.

This is a time for traditional hand-fastings ancient woodland weddings which took place and bound two people together for a year and a day. Weddings are still very popular at this time even today, and the significance behind the wedding ring is that of an unbroken circle of vows and of life.

Our May Queen would have been proud to have been chosen
to represent her village in this way. The Sun is in the zodiac
sign of Taurus, which is ruled by Venus, the goddess of beauty,
abundance, growth and harvest. Young girls would bathe
their faces with the early morning dew for everlasting beauty.
Sycamore wood used for love spoons, love advice and spells was
the name of the game as thoughts turned to finding partners for
the dance of creation ... the Maypole was, and still is, central to
this festival!

the may dance

A tall pole anchored in the ground, connecting the earth and the sky, and with two colours of ribbons attached to the top. Flowers and greenery are all around as this is a festival of fertility.

The alchemy of our journey around the wheel of the year reaches a time when we look for the marriage of two becoming a third. The ribbons are woven into a pattern by the dance. Lots of ribbons. Boys and girls, men and women - all represented by the two colours of ribbon. And the dance weaves the colours together, circling and moving between each other as the ribbons get shorter and the maypole becomes two colours intertwined.

Take a moment to picture the dancing in your mind's eye and, maybe, even hear the music playing. The bonfires would be lit, and food brought as merriment ensued through the evening.

And in your own celebration or ritual for Beltane, watch for those little nudges from the Universe or even from the goddess Venus herself. As you extend your hands outward in order to grow, observe that this is the festival for growth on levels and THE festival of love.

the season of little summer

From Beltane, we will work our way through May and on into June towards the Summer Solstice - however, every season has its significance for us in different ways, and this one, sitting opposite the darkest point of the year, revels in light!

There is an astrological term 'applying', which is where two planetary bodies are moving towards an aspect. They may well be getting close to each other, becoming conjunct (next), or moving into a position of opposition, trine or square with another. Whatever they are up to, it will be something of note. And so we say a planet (or star) is applying when the pattern of energy created is becoming stronger.

And we can see this in nature and, particularly, right now in our wheel of the year. Spring is applying to Summer and transforming the energy from green shoots into plants to be nurtured into full maturity. And so this new season beckons us outside and into an energetic life force all around us!

festivals & 'ho' to the sun

There are other festivals of celebration at this time, and all will honour bounty and abundance - it is particularly significant to look out for flower festivals. Villages still decorate entrance gates to their churches and wells. As you're out and about, take time to see where flowers are being used to make things pretty! Farmers markets begin to emerge, and this, again, has traditions going back to times of taking produce to market. Selling, buying, growing early crops and celebrating that we are provided for!

And, as another nod to the opposite festival of Samhain, you might see pretty flower wreaths on doors or even feel like creating one yourself. If you do, be sure to ask permission of the flowers and the foliage if using from the hedgerows and heed if the answer is no. The plants and flowers know their destiny and purpose, and so it is a very special thing to ask a plant and have that inner feeling that it wants to share some time with you!

May is usually when the Chelsea Flower Show is held in London by the Royal Horticultural Society. It is open over several days and shows flowers, often new varieties, garden designs and structures. It is innovative and yet with history too. And, as it is filmed, we can all delight in the colours of Springtime displayed at their very best.

From formal dances to markets and open gardens, the Little Summer has opportunities for us all to rejoice in our beautiful home planet Earth!

notes from the ancestors

The story of a brass bowl.

It has been in our family for as long as I can remember. Nan polished it, and it lived on her dresser, and it was the only thing she had of her real Mother. It's big, measuring around 8 inches at the top and probably about 12 inches in the 'bulb' part of the bowl. The top is pretty ...

So our family tree has a short branch with my Nan. We know very little about her real Mother as she died giving birth to Nan. Nan's father married again, and he died soon after the wedding, so there were no step-siblings for Nan. My Great Grandma was left to bring up Nan, who was not her child by blood, in the very early years of the 1900s. By all accounts, it was a happy relationship, and, in later years, my Dad would go and visit Great Grandma (as she was known) regularly - which means I heard so much about her in addition to our family visits. I know they talked about Spiritualism, which, given the complicated family tree, is interesting. Nan was not related to her by blood and yet was taught to read the tea leaves and became well known in her village for her predictions ... the family we choose!

Have I told you yet about my Dad? He was a platform medium in the spiritualist church until my Mum stopped him ...

The Brass Bowl. It had been passed down to Nan's real mother. So it is, most likely, Victorian. It's old, and we really don't know how old. The brass is thin in parts, and I polish it now with great care.

And, when polished, it is highly reflective, like a mirror. A face reflected in the gentle reddish-gold colour becomes beautiful, much like in candlelight. How many faces have been visible on the surface of the bowl? My earliest memories of scrying were not in fire but in the surface of that bowl.

I have the memory of Nan polishing her brass bowl and filling it with dried flowers and, in December, with foliage and fruits. Only much later did I realise the significance of her seasonal display! And I continue the ritual with a vase that fits the bowl for fresh flowers and dried - I'm as careful with the inside as the outside.

Psychometry is the art of tuning into an object's history, which can be useful, although, for my brass bowl, I do know quite a bit already! However, when polishing it, I let my mind drift as I'm touching the bowl and sense Nan sitting at her table looking out over the garden and watching Grandad Ted. And before that, in the small terraced house where they brought Mum up.

- **Scrying** - letting the eyes go out of focus and the imagination offers us images or feelings from our extra senses. This is great to do with an outside campfire and to look into the heart of burning logs - remember there is, cannot be, any right or wrong with what you sense!

- **Ritual** - I clear the table and cover it with newspaper. Brass cleaner and cloths at the ready, and I polish the bowl. This takes me time and care. The bowl is big, and as I rotate it, it takes concentration to make sure all of the surface is gleaming and shiny. I wash the vase that fits inside and dry it carefully. I line the bottom of the bowl with kitchen paper. And then, it is time to arrange a display of flowers and foliage for the season. This takes me, perhaps, a whole afternoon and calms and inspires me.

And Nan's brass bowl connects me with the female line of my ancestors.

being

There are so many wonderful ways to celebrate this time and to bring a deeper awareness for yourself through doing so.

Weaving. Bread can be baked with plaited dough, wool crocheted into a drinks coaster or make your own maypole complete with ribbons - your intention here is to celebrate nature and her ability to transform and grow.

Intentions are key at this magical time of the year ...

Intention - what you want an action, word or thought to represent.

Symbolism - an item, drawing or saying that represents something else.

As you weave ribbons or wool together, be aware of your thoughts and intentions, as that is where the real Beltane magic lives. Weave your own ancestral magic with each turn of ribbon and absorb yourself in something quite ancient.

Flax

Flax takes 100 days to grow, and the beginning of May is a traditional time for the seeds to be planted. It is sown directly into the soil and grows to its best potential when surrounded by a flax community. Flax likes the company of other flax plants, and they will prop each other up. There is so much we can learn from the flax plants, and, of course, nature really does have so much wisdom to offer us when we look and listen.

Our ancestors grew flax to transform it into textiles and, through the regenerative movement towards sustainable textiles, which is becoming more mainstream, thank goodness, we can take part in the amazing process of taking a seed all the way through from planting to making cloth. As a craft, it reminds us of the connections between nature and the material.

As we tend the plants, we realise we are looking after that which looks after us.

The seeds we plant have within themselves to become their best potential ... or not. They choose whether to germinate and grow, and there is something quite humble in growing a natural plant without chemicals or any kind of genetic manipulation.

*The seed will decide on the purpose,
and we are merely the nurturer.*

You may not live in an area where you could take on the challenge of growing a metre square of flax and then harvesting and spinning; however, do check out the Fibershed Movement as the more we think about where our clothes and textiles come from, the more we can positively affect our planet's ecosystem as we move forwards!

doing

Beltane is also known as the cleansing time. Herbs were thrown onto the bonfires, and the smoke was used to cleanse animals. In my research over the years into the festivals, I've always found overlapping of certain traditions and different areas doing things in different months.

And, perhaps, it's a great time for our own cleaning, too ... especially as we're about to be going out and about meeting people! So could you arrange a detox for yourself? Or some form of cleansing ritual to breathe in the new air of potential and to feel that sense of newness?

Experiment with your intentions to surround yourself with a bubble of light. Here is my version for you. It is so quick that you can do this while brushing your teeth, and, actually, it's something I recommend. If you can get into the habit of grounding and connecting, plus surrounding yourself with a bubble of light at tooth brushing time, then it becomes a habit made!

A Fresh Start to the Day

Be aware of your breath in and out - don't change it, and just breathe naturally.
From your tailbone (not so long ago, we had tails, you know!), take that wonderful awareness down into the Earth and stretch right down to the centre of the Earth.
that grounds you
Then, visualise (no need to close your eyes) a bubble of gorgeous and beautiful light all around you, almost as if you were inside a transparent egg.

And clap your hands in celebration of being you!

playing

What a lovely month for us to be playing outside, and I would say, first and foremost, go outside and play!! As I write this and think about the maypole dancing, I wonder whether 'ring a ring of roses' is related as nursery rhymes tend to have their origins way back in our history. Mind you, that particular one may also have a darker element due to posies being worn to cover up the smell from people who had the plague in 1665 London. I've digressed …

Back to sweet-smelling flowers coloured ribbons, and could you go out of your garden and find a local flower festival? They will be around at this time to celebrate all that is growing.

And, whilst we're looking at the wonderful plants and flowers, this would be a great time to practice seeing their auras.

Sit comfortably in front of a plant, tree, flower or even fruit bush. Make sure you're safe to do this, as you will be letting your eyes go slightly out of focus. Always stop if you feel at all uncomfortable in any way!

And so ... you are in front of something living, and you already know that there will be an energetic aura of some description or other. Let your eyes go slightly out of focus and have curiosity and awe as you gently look at the leaf or whatever you choose. You may see a slight change in the light around it. You may see colours. There might be movement.

Or you may just find that you feel a little more tranquil and calm!

Just do this for a few moments and record whatever you saw, felt, imagined, heard or how you feel afterwards!

This is in our 'Playing' section as it's a fun thing to do, and, who knows, you may find new thoughts are inspired.

To honour the time you spent there, say 'thank you'.

stillness

We live on a magical planet and one that, even now, we really don't fully understand!

And so, for the stillness in May, we bring the balance of the inner and outer for ourselves and for our planet.

- By sitting still and quiet, we give the Earth time for restoration.
- By breathing gently and calmly, we give the Earth time to restore.
- By allowing some time to pass where we ask no more from the Earth than some air and a place for us to sit, we give the Earth time to rest.

As you begin to occupy more space on the Earth again, it is a lovely thing to ask if the land around you would like a song.

Hum quietly and give the music and air to the land or the sea. Spending time like this is so special and full of wonder for us in ways that I couldn't even write for you ... but you can!

dear friend

Dear friend,

In the season of Little Summer, begun at the festival of Beltane, we're out. Outside, dancing and enjoying that life has returned to our neighbourhoods and communities. Did you watch a dance of ribbons or make your own?

As I walk beside you or dance along, perhaps we could muse as to what our alchemists of old would make of all of the amazing inventions we have now. Whether we hear music played live in front of us or through a screen, the musicians have created something very special for us in their moment of creation.

Before we move gracefully into the next turn of the wheel of the year, I invite you to flick back through the pages of Little

Summer and note which ideas, thoughts, stories, practises and celebrations resonated.

Did my story of Nan's brass bowl bring a memory to the surface of something that your own ancestors did to welcome each season? Or, if we accept the concept of time not linear, are you instilling a ritual of seasonal observance into your lineage?

Shall we dance into Summer?

Together?

As always, with love from Alison x

summer

Winter Solstice /
Yule

Halloween/
Samhain

Imbolc

Autumn Equinox /
Harvest

Spring Equinox /
Ostara

Lammas /
Harvest

Beltane /
May Day

Summer Solstice /
Midsummer

summer - june & july

Summer Solstice and the Sun are at the opposite point to Winter Solstice. Both Solstices are the mystically transformational times of the year as they open gateways to change light itself and, quite literally, illuminate our navigation into a new half of the year.

The energy is transforming on all levels.

The rhythm of our Earth has shown me so many times that the two Solstice points are the 'when' we can raise our vibration through choosing to use the gift of transformation. The Sun stands still at Solstice and prepares to alter the balance, or, probably more accurately, our Earth and the Sun reach a different alignment and a change of energy.

At a date in the middle of June (usually around the 19th - 23rd), the Sun will move from the zodiac constellation of Gemini into Cancer. The point of movement into Cancer, the 0°, is the Summer Solstice and heralds the longest day with the most daylight. And it represents the time when hours of daylight will begin to slowly lessen and the nights draw in.

And yet ...

This is also the time for harvest to begin and the crops to be nourished and nurtured into maturity ...

grounding & connecting

How are you getting on with making grounding and connecting a part of your daily routine? Throughout the chapters, I'm offering slightly different versions of what is, actually, my own practice built up over years and used in many groups, workshops and yurts! We're all unique and have our own peculiar inner languages, ways to listen to our bodies and missions involving life on this planet, so please adapt these 'Grounding and Connecting' ideas to suit your own inner language and circumstances.

Summer Solstice Grounding and Connection

Take a moment to sense where you are by standing (or sitting) still and reach your awareness down through your tailbone to the ground beneath and then further down until you sense the centre of the Earth.

Connect to the Earth.

And then expand your awareness out to the sky above your head and the infinity of the universe and space.

Connected to the Earth and the Universe.

Tuning your frequency into the Earth and the Universe.

And then feel the horizon of our planet stretching out from either side of you and in front and behind and all around you.

This is a great time to reinforce your bubble of light all around you too ...

Summer Solstice, high Summer, represents that time when the Sun is bright and crops are at their most bountiful.

Raise your hands up to the sky and then slowly take them down to touch the earth.

Stand up straight and tall, and be proud of the wonderful human you are.

And now you are grounded and tuned in to your own connected frequency of the Universe itself - magical!!

summer solstice / litha

Each of the festivals celebrates the turning wheel of the year and has individual energies as one season becomes another. The two Solstices are a true transformation of light and dark, and now we, in our calendar, have reached the Summer Solstice. Beltane, the Maytime dancing and feasts marked the beginning of Summer, and our crops are ripening and produce becomes more abundant. We are in Mid-summer, and this festival time is also known as Litha, and it's the busiest of times. Remember, your ancestors would have been working hard in the fields, tending the crops, making what was needed and generally taking care of what had been created.

And that's what it's about.

That's what this time is about.

Nurturing and nourishing that which will provide for our future.

The Sun enters the sign of Cancer, and we celebrate creation and the sustainability of us ... ourselves ... our self ... our loved ones ... our wider world ...

Interestingly, the zodiac sign of Cancer is ruled by the Moon, and so, at this time of welcoming the Sun moving into Cancer, we are also honouring our Moon too! In case I haven't mentioned it already, it is my deeply held belief that we are such a lucky planet. We have the Sun to provide warmth and light and help us in our quest for living. And our moon is only ours as no other planet has our moon as their own and gives us a rhythm to the water table, the seas, our imagination, and so much more.

And then there's something else that we see in nature. Each petal on a flower, every ear of corn - they all lead their lives in the way they want to because nothing that nature produces will be the same. Leaves and flowers may look similar, but they'll all be very different. Each has a unique energy, potential, and purpose.

And that's something else you might want to bring into your own idea of how to celebrate this time - by being uniquely you! Have some fun, be creative, imaginative, and just love life. And then let's see that energy ripple outwards in the true nature of the Summer ... the world would be a brilliant place if everybody just celebrated!

festivals & 'ho' to the sun

There are other festivals of celebration at this time, and all will be honouring the switch between the longest day of the Solstice and moving us into the days pulling the light in. You will find mid-summer dances, pilgrimages to walk to stone circles, gathering points and music festivals, all celebrating that this season begins with the longest day.

It is worthwhile visiting an ancient site in June for the Solstice as, highly likely, there will be a ceremony held to mark this time. And, as with all of the festivals, there is a ripple of celebrations that take place throughout June and July. From the July 4th Independence Day celebrations through to those held on village greens, fetes and carnivals, the overarching theme is that of life and joy!

Glastonbury Festival of Music is usually held just after the Solstice, and I spent many years working as an astrologer there. If you went during the late '90s and the '00s and visited the Green Futures field, you may well have had a tarot or birth chart reading from me!

morris dancing

Morris dancing is a traditional form of dance seen, particularly in England and parts of Europe, at festivals in the Spring and Summer. Usually performed by all-male groups, there are sometimes women now taking up the roles, and I was so lucky to see this. The men tend to wear all white, and the women either white or blue - the colours of the Moon and the Moon Goddess. Wearing bells on their ankles, they will carry a red or white handkerchief and sticks of wood.

Every single step in a Morris Dance has something to say symbolically, and the whole dance will tell a story.

The pieces of wood celebrate the agricultural tools of the trade. And, by clicking the sticks together and waving the handkerchiefs at each other, a battle of light & dark is enacted. It's not such a leap to believe that, at some point in history, swords would have been used symbolising the battles, which has evolved into much safer and symbolic gestures.

It's all about honouring tradition and carrying these stories through.

Some of the dances of the Morris dancers honour the connection with the earth and with the sky. And, when we have that connection of the Earth and the sky, so we feel in alignment. A Morris dance will recognise our position in time and space and in culture and history.

Surround yourself with the colours of abundance and beauty. Look to nature and the hedgerows and see the natural colours of yellow, gold, pink, and green. The bees are buzzing in flowers, and the fruit is ripening on trees and bushes.

And dance …

oak king & holly king

We first met these two Kings in the chapter of Yule & Winter Solstice.

And they are about to go into battle again!

Who will wear the crown this time?

Our strong Oak King has worked hard since December to inspire growth with meaning and purpose and has ruled impeccably since the Winter Solstice. Oak brings his produce, lessons learned, spirit of travel and new offspring to the battle.

And yet the Holly King, with his evergreen foliage, offers the gift of time to withdraw and to give the earth some respite. Holly will provide greenery in the face of dark and cold. His vibrant red berries will offer hope of warmth to come as we deepen into the cooler, darker half of the year.

The Sun will begin to abandon us ... at least, that's how it would have seemed to our ancestors!

The battle commences for the crown, and the Holly King is determined to regain the crown from Oak. Oak is determined to hold onto his crown and rule for more months. Holly King has nature at his side this time, though, as the leaves will fall to make space for new, and the Earth will want her to sleep.

And he does it!

Holly King will wear his crown of berries for the next half of the year. His responsibilities are immense as he will bring understanding that all times pass and, indeed, there will be warmer times ahead after we get through the coming Winter and the darker months. However, until we meet the two Kings again at the next Solstice and Winter, we will move through Summer and Autumn with all the celebrations, beauty, new understandings and rest for what is ahead.

the solstice & stone circles

Have you visited a stone circle? There is a sense of mystery and connection with the ancestors of our ancestors. At Solstices particularly, people will gather at burial chambers, on high points, and at other ancient monuments and stone circles.

Even after thousands of years of our earth turning and the planets moving, there will still be an incredible spectacle of the Sun beaming its light in a certain way year after year inside a stone circle. Are they calendars and places for rituals? Or perhaps meeting places ...

The phenomenal structures, especially Stonehenge, are huge, and so the building of them is incredibly difficult for us to comprehend just how they were constructed. Likewise, the Pyramids in Egypt - how were they built to be so perfect? We would struggle with the geometry even with all of our machinery and knowledge these days. How would we build such structures? But they were built, and it opens our minds to the one-ness of the universe and the wonders of the earth to ponder on these powerful forms on our landscapes.

Stone circles are mainly found in Britain, Ireland and some parts of France. I will say 'mainly' as their origin is ancient, and we still don't really know exactly how they were built and for what purposes. The stones used for Stonehenge, for instance, are well documented as being brought to the site from as far away as South Wales - a long way to transport huge stones at the time before mechanised transport. And in the Salisbury Museum, there are Stonehenge artefacts showing links to much further afield. There must have been such a reliance on trade routes for passing information along, and that deserves complete respect.

Usually, there will be a correlation between a gap in the stone circle, a centre mound or a stone set apart (known as a Standing Stone), and a Solstice sunrise or sunset. It is mind-blowing and a testament to the knowledge our ancestors knew that the Sun will still, even now, shine on a particular spot or stone.

Whenever you go, please allow time to dwell, ponder and connect with the Earth's energy of these places. They hold ancestral memories of the people who have collected there over thousands of years. And, using your extra senses, you may even tune into them or the land. Maybe you will see, hear, feel, gain messages from, or even pass messages to the stones for future people to find!

my hebridean / callanish story

The moon pausing her travels over the sleeping beauty.

Moon, Photo credit - Terry Smith

In 2006, I travelled to Callanish in the Hebrides, Scotland, to see a major Lunar standstill. Callanish is a magical and very 'other-worldly' place with standing stones and an incredibly dramatic stone circle. The lunar standstill is a phenomenon of the Moon which only takes place every 18-19 years or so, and for the June 2006 Major Lunar Standstill, I was part of a wonderful group of astrologers who travelled to Callanish in the Hebrides to be at one of the most awesome and inspiring of Stone Circles in order to experience the 'event' in the fullest way we could.

To watch the Moon appear to a standstill whilst standing on the earth in the site of standing stones and stone circles was a powerful connection and one I've never forgotten. It was like plugging myself into a high frequency circuit board!

Visiting a stone circle is quite breathtaking, and if you are able to, please do. I've dowsed for the energy of many of them, and some of the strongest I found was at the Rollright Stones in Warwickshire/Oxfordshire. These date back to Neolithic times (probably!) and are located over two sites, which, when you walk between them, have an incredible sense of walking through history and into another time!

Standing Stone, Photo credit - Terry Smith

notes from the ancestors

The story of my Dad and his guide.

My Dad was the youngest of four children and was born in Plymouth in, Devon. He joined the army at age 15 as a mechanical engineer just after World War 2. So he was involved in rebuilding works in Europe, worked on tanks and other vehicles in Malaya and probably other mechanical work in places that I can't remember!

My memories of his memories and the stories that he told were mostly of the camaraderie he experienced amongst his regiment, and I suspect this was brilliant for a young lad away from home. He mended vehicles, understood how they worked and was a very practical man.

He met and married my Mum in 1960. Although he frequently told me about this, he had a life-changing experience between leaving the army and his marriage.

At some point in the late 1950s, he stayed for a few months on the Isle of Rùm, which is one of the smaller of the Hebridean islands off the west coast of Scotland. The landscape is rugged and beautiful, and the whole island is very sparsely populated. The Hebrides are beautiful, and I stayed on the Isle of Lewis & Harris in 2006 for the very rare Lunar standstill as you've just read! However, back to the 1950s, when my Dad met his spirit guide.

He (my dad) was walking one day on Rùm, and an old man, in spirit, just appeared by his side. Dad called him the Old Man of Rùm and said he had a beard, used very colourful language, and with whom he had long, in-depth conversations.

They continued to talk and work together all through Dad's life, although, as time went on, Dad talked about him less but never completely stopped mentioning him to me, so I know he was with Dad when he died. My Dad died in 1981, aged 55, which was no age at all, and I was there with him as he passed. I'm feeling sad as I write this as he had so much still to offer this world; however, I also know that he is mending things, or people, somewhere else just now.

The Old Man of Rùm helped my Dad with his mediumship and platform work.

Platform work is when a medium stands in front of a group of people and channels through messages from those who

have passed. It's a particular gift and one which Dad nor I ever questioned, as it is something like an extra sense and as natural as hearing or seeing. Probably because he was so practical and down to earth; it just was something else he did. My Dad also wrote stories and screenplays - one of my best memories is of him chain-smoking and tapping away on his typewriter into the small hours every night in the attic room next to my bedroom. We didn't know then what we know now about smoking!
He wrote stories about people and really understood that the characters drove the stories. He was also a prolific reader and went to the library for his four books every week - anything with an adventure story. People - it was always about people with my Dad!

Our gifts. We all have different gifts and things we do better. For instance, I am most definitely not an artist, but I can draw pin-stick people. I am not a cake baker, but I can cook curries. I am not a medium of platform standard but have channelled through messages from the spirit world. I'm extremely intuitive, an astrologer and a Tarot expert. My extra senses of sight and audio are acute and at a high frequency. I understand symbolism as a language, and it all makes sense to me.

I'd love you to take a moment right now and think or write ...

I am not a/an ... but I can ...

When my Dad didn't have a tool for a task, he would make one, and another great memory I have is of him working away in our cellar, making something of use. We lived in an odd house at that time because it had a coal cellar and also attic rooms and yet was the smaller part of a big house with twisting and turning staircases. My Dad had the type of mind that could work things out with logic and also had the strong imagination to write stories. I always suspected that he was behind the letters I received when I was very young from the fairies …

There are several ways to get in touch with your spirit guides, animal guides and even your ancestral guides. The realms around us all are busy, and the absolutely best advice I can give is to wait and see who comes towards you. If it is someone or something that you feel instinctively will be of help in your pathway forward, then begin the conversation in whatever language is apt. And say 'no' to anyone or anything that isn't best serving you at the time.

My Dad knew that the Old man of Rùm was his guide. He absolutely knew it. And that, together with things my Grandad said to me, enforced the knowledge inside of me that when we really know, so we really know, and it is.

Take a step towards that knowing right now by looking outside at the Moon and knowing it is our moon. Take hold of a stone or piece of wood and say to yourself that 'you know' it is what it is. Something happens in our brain as we tune into the 'knowing' in that we want to know more!

For Peter, my Dad, with love,
Thank you, Dad - you gave me such an
amazing start in this lifetime.

being

Wearing white at this time is wonderful because white is one of the colours of Summer Solstice. White is a feminine goddess colour and celebrates life.

There are so many wonderful ways to join in with the Solstice and the Summer energy, and this is to give you some ideas. Remember that we are welcoming in a new six-week (or so) season, so you don't have to do this all at once!

There is a great moment for a body re-alignment, however, if you do decide to watch the sunrise on the Solstice morning. We are, through our ancestral memories, tuned in to the frequency of the Solstices particularly, and I do recommend being present during a Solstice if you can.

Have you tried making tea from fresh herbs from the garden or even the store? Take some peppermint leaves and steep in 'just boiled' water. Or another herb like chamomile or even sage. Check that the herb is as it says it is, make sure it's safe for you, and always start with a small amount, as some herbs (I'm thinking mint here) can be strong!

Strawberries. We tend to think of strawberries around the time of Wimbledon in the UK and serving them with cream! Strawberries are powerful and symbolic for this time because they are best when fresh, grown outside and ripened in the sun. They don't freeze very well as they tend towards mushiness on thawing! But there is also something about eating fruit and the sweetness and ripeness of the fruit to celebrate life.

Can you watch a Summer sunrise?
With all of the potential of the day ahead?

doing

Spirit Guides. This is a subject worthy of a book of its own, however, and for the months of June and July, we will concentrate on our guides inspired by nature. There will be more about guides in our Samhain chapter, I promise you!

Find a place in which you sense history and a resonance with yourself. It may be a wood, stone circle, beach, your garden, a special bench or just a place outdoors where you feel safe and loved.

Be awake and aware for this as it's not a meditation or visualisation. Listen to the birds and feel the air around you. Let nature surround you, and have an intention of meeting a guide. When your guide is ready to step forward, they will do so. And please do not worry if it's not today ... you've already signalled to your highest self, your ancestors and the universe that you are ready. Let your guide catch up with you and, when he, she, they or it does ...

Ask them for their name.

Question them just as you would a new person who has entered your world.

Will they become a friend? What do they have to offer you? What can you offer them?

This is a great start to writing a new story of you and your guide. And, as I mentioned above, give it time!

playing

Think of the word 'Flamboyance', and it's close to how we are going to play today! Bright colours alert!

Using a hoop of wood (or wire), wrap ribbons all around and, especially, make sure any jagged edges or splinters are covered and made safe with brightly coloured ribbons of all the colours. And then decorate some more with flowers and streamers and good luck tokens ... anything that speaks to your inner language of joy, love and celebration. Twirl it around and use it for decoration, either inside or outside the home!

Another way of making a record of the Solstice to take into the darker months is to make a pendant for yourself from clay or to paint a stone. Use the colours for the Sun and the Moon of Gold and Silver, and remember to think about your intentions for the season whilst thanking the Sun for having brought such bounty to us.

Creating Gold

And next, we're going to create gold! At least we're giving it the opportunity to show up in our lives. Please go out into the world and find five beautiful smooth stones. Wash them and let them dry. Paint them gold, and here's the alchemically important part: as you do so, visualise what gold you'd like to bring into your home. Remember, in Beltane, we used intention in weaving, and now we use it as we paint our stones.

It may help to ask yourself what 'gold' means to you. It may well be increased abundance in some way or wealth or good vibrations. Our inner gold that the alchemists of old searched for (and probably still do) is uniquely different for each of us!

- **Attraction** - bringing something towards
- **Manifestation** - something appears as if out of nowhere.

By the way, I've always found it quite interesting that gold paint tends to take longer to dry than other colours, and I've no idea why! Please allow time for this, especially as you'll need to turn the stones over to ensure they are fully gold.

When they are fully painted gold, shiny and prepared with their intention, you will need to find a place for them to work their manifestation magic. If you place them by the front door (for gold within the home), place them to the right-hand side as you look at the door from outside. Whether indoors or outside, make sure that the energy flows freely and isn't hampered by a corner or wall, etc! Move them around to really 'feel' into where is best - you'll know!

Energy needs to flow always, so polish them, give them a pamper session or just move them around every now and again, as we don't want cobwebs forming around our gold! Maybe this will work and maybe not; however, I'm firmly of the opinion that an action has a reaction ... somewhere!

stillness

For this section, we have a visualisation for Summer.

So just sit comfortably and remember to breathe. This is not a long meditation or anything like that; it is just to help you start to get that preparation in place for moving through Solstice and on into Summer.

And just have in mind a seashell on a beautiful seashore.

There is sand, and there are stones. You hear the sea and the waves gently in the background.

On the sand in front of you, there is a circle drawn. It may be outlined by stones or driftwood or just drawn. It's your circle, so please design it in your mind however you'd like it to look. There may even be seaweed around it!

And, as you're sitting there, the sea begins to come in, and the waves start to wash your circle away …

And now there's nothing there. Just the seashore … and yet … you see … just by your feet … a piece of driftwood …

As you pick it up, open your mind to a thought or a word or a sense of something new arriving

In your mind's eye, you stand up tall and straight and throw the driftwood as far as you can into the sea.

That's what I want to send out into the world.

Thank the sand and the sea and open your eyes if they were closed.

You've been still and active.

And now you're prepared for the Summer ahead.

dear friend

Dear friend,

Summer has opened her arms and proclaimed that the Sun is high in the sky, the crops are ripening, Wimbledon has begun, and music is played outside. Did you see a sunrise around the time of the Solstice? Or maybe you heard some drums playing in the distance as the light half of the year became, gently, the darker half. The fairies are said to dance on Mid-Summer eve, and there is magic all around. Magic is there at all times for us when we look and ask, and yet, on certain days or nights, we may be able to sense it more.

Before we move gracefully into the next turn of the wheel of the year, I invite you to flick back through the pages of this chapter and note which ideas, thoughts, stories, practises and celebrations resonated. I wonder whether you met your spirit guide or maybe an animal came towards you with a message. Perhaps your own unique inner language tuned you into scents or colours as prompts for insights.

Did you dance and have fun?

I'm by your side as we gently sway towards our next festival time and season of Lammas and the little harvest!

As always, with love from Alison x

harvest

Winter Solstice /
Yule

Halloween/
Samhain

Imbolc

Autumn Equinox /
Harvest

Spring Equinox /
Ostara

Lammas /
Harvest

Beltane /
May Day

Summer Solstice /
Midsummer

harvest - august & september

Lammastide and the Sun are high in the sky with crops ripened and ready to begin the harvest. There would have been, still is, the constant mantra of "What is ripe?" Or "What is ready to eat?"

The festival of Lammas is an agricultural festival and is celebrated when the time was ready, usually around the first of August. As we saw with the Beltane celebrations, each festival would take place on a day when work could be put to one side. It's an outdoor party with a bonfire, and so we need a day with no rain. And, lastly, it had to be arranged for just as harvest had begun … and there is a very real symbolic reason for that.

I'd like us to remind ourselves of the rhythm of the year cycle and see where this festival fits in!

February and Imbolc with the first milk available from animals, the first sign of green appearing in our gardens and fields. And then we move to mid-March and the Spring Equinox / Ostara with equal light and dark. The beginning of May brings Beltane and May Day and a time to celebrate everything that's fertile, abundant and social. Then June with her Summer solstice, mid-summer and the crops are growing and ripening.

And now we get to this festival in August of Lammas and the early harvest ...

grounding & connecting

Ready to come back to earth and ground to connect, tune in and align ourselves with the rhythm of the Universe?

The Solstice was quite a heady time and a jolt to the system if we observed the sunrise with the realisation that the longest day of the year was taking place and the light has transformed. The season drew the light in so subtly, and it is only now, as we move through August and then on into September, that we will notice the changing light.

Take a moment to sense where you are by standing (or sitting) still and reach your awareness down through your tailbone to the ground beneath and then further down until you sense the centre of the Earth.

Connect to the Earth.

And then expand your awareness out to the sky above your head and the infinity of the universe and space.

Connected to the Earth and the Universe.

Tuning your frequency into the Earth and the Universe.

And then feel the horizon of our planet stretching out from either side of you, in front and behind and all around you.

Visualise the bounty of nature all around - the energy from the plants, trees, crops and wildlife. Reinforce your bubble of light all around you and know that you are at one with your body and the body of the earth and universe.

Raise your hands up to the sky and then slowly take them down to touch the earth.

Stand up straight and tall, and be proud of the wonderful human you are.

And now you are grounded, tuned in to your own connected frequency of the Universe itself and ready to celebrate nature in all her magnificence!!

lammas

August heralds the festival of Harvest with the first loaf of bread made with the new crop of grain - a time to give thanks for the bounty provided by nature.

The colours are of ripening crops and fruits with their reds and oranges. Everything's getting ready for harvest. Flowers are abundant in nature, and the hedgerows are full of wildlife.

There is passion and joyfulness all around us, and it's a noisy time! Lammas is an agricultural festival, and so doesn't rely on a particular astrological time, although during the month of July, we will have seen the sun move from the zodiac sign of Cancer into Leo. Cancer is ruled by the Moon, and then Leo is ruled by the Sun. There is something very ancient as a thread to ponder on with this time of beginning to get the crops in from the fields and the astrology turning from a sign ruled by the Moon into a sign ruled by the sun. And yet, it's all about the farms, crops and nature. I'll return to the zodiac in a while as it's time for us to see how the constellations have, all through ages, given us a sense of this calendar we are gradually getting to know through this book.

Lammas is also known, in the Celtic tradition, as Lughnasadd and the Feast of the Sun god 'Llugh' celebrating all aspects of life, death and rebirth.

It's traditional at this time to make a corn dolly from the first corn that's harvested and to keep it as the seed for next year's sowing. There's the cycle again of life itself. Harvest the corn and keep some back as seeds for the next year.

And so we think about our feast and what will be on the table. Through the month of August and into September, we will be outside working hard, so freshly baked bread is a staple food. Also ready now are berries for juice, salad crops and anything else easy to pick and eat straight away. Another change of astrological sign is when the Sun moves from Leo and into Virgo around the 21st of August.

There's a mystical and symbolic side to every single festival, and we will light fires in the evening to celebrate, to enjoy life and to extend our day.

August is also a time when crop circles occur in fields, and there are mysteries surrounding them. The term 'crop circle' was first coined in the 1980s; however, sightings go back much further to the phenomenon and may have been recorded as far back as the 1600s. Are they made by people from Earth or from somewhere else? Some crop circles are so intricate that it is difficult to work out how they're made, and, more often than not, there will be some form of zodiac connotation. And so, let's consider the constellations and signs of the zodiac for a moment.

the zodiac

When we were born, there was made a particular pattern of stars in the sky, which is absolutely unique for each of us. Our current style of displaying the birth chart, a map of the stars for that moment of arrival on Earth, is as two circles with one inside the other. The central circle represents the earth and our position on it. Over to the right and left of our position would be the horizon. Then, the outer circle fills in the picture of where the planetary bodies were in relation to the horizon at the time. A noon birth will show the Sun above the horizon, whereas a midnight birth will show the Sun below.

The position of the constellations is also shown around the outer edge of the birth chart. And so, for a noon birth, the Sun will be above the horizon and in the particular sign of the zodiac for the time of year.

The birth chart becomes a wheel with the signs of the zodiac in order and stretching out around our self standing on the middle circle of Earth. We've already thought about how our universe doesn't comply with our Gregorian calendar. You'll need to consult a reliable ephemeris to find out just where the Sun, Moon and other planetary bodies are in the different signs of the zodiac.

I see nature and the Universe as cycles and rhythms, and, unless we're drawing up an exact chart for a time of birth or specific event, we can bask in the warmth and creativity of each zodiac sign and the planets said for a thousand years so to rule them, as they relate to our turning wheel of the year and our celebrations of nature and our earth.

Each of the signs of the zodiac is associated with one of the four elements of Earth, Air, Fire and Water. These are our building blocks of astrology and also of life, and as we work to further our own knowledge of the elements, signs and planets (including our own!) so, we gain in our alignment and our sense of how we fit into the amazing puzzle of life on this planet.

the signs

Aries - March into April

Our energetic pioneer

The Sun moves into the sign of Aries, Spring Equinox, and equals the amount of light and dark. This is just the shock that the earth needs to wake up and begin to grow again. As the Sun moves through this sign, we can feel the setting in place of energies for the coming year.

The element of Fire is very obvious for Aries as it is ruled by Mars and holds great energy to move the Earth into action. Mars doesn't hold back and, as the ancient Roman god of war, will move, shake and generally make certain that actions are taken, beginnings are begun, and the phrase 'a force of nature' is enacted.

Aries is our first sign of the Zodiac and, like the dawning of a new day, has all of the creative potential for the year ahead and the desire to make things happen.

Taurus - April into May

Earth to Universe

Taurus is of the element Earth and quickly, most definitely, brings a sense of realism to what has been started. Routines, security in knowing what task needs doing next, regularity and purpose. And yet, as the Sun travels through Taurus, we are also invited to consider the connection of Earth and the heavens. In the Tarot deck, Taurus is represented as the Hierophant, the Pope or High Priest, and this tells us more about this part of the year.

Taurus energy connects the Earth and what we are planting and growing with spirit. The material with the spiritual. No wonder then that the Maypole dance fits beautifully and symbolically in the middle of this sign.

This is one of two signs of the zodiac ruled by planet Venus in her role as goddess of nature and abundance, and she brings the inspiration to ensure growth and beauty.

Gemini - May into June

Inspiring Potential

Gemini is ruled by planet Mercury and is associated with the element of Air. The mercurial spirit of fun, tricks, talking, chatting, and intelligence makes this the sign where our connections with other people become apparent. As we talk to each other, we are passing on knowledge and news. As the plants take root and grow upwards, they are communicating through the air and with birds and bees.

The glyph symbol for this sign is of 'two' or 'twins', and this bears great wisdom as the weather will often turn quickly from warm to cold and dry to rain. It isn't a stable weather and yet brings just what nature needs. And so the sense of Gemini month is about giving the plants exactly the conditions they need to thrive. We even see frosts occasionally and can, and I've pondered on this a lot, mimic the turn of the season from Winter into Spring. A quick freeze and then a warm morning inspiring more seeds far underground to wake up and realise their potential.

Cancer - June into July

Our Nurturer of all

The sign of Cancer is ruled by the Moon, and yet, as we have already seen in this book, heralds one of the two most crucial astrological Solar festivals. As the Sun enters the constellation of Cancer, our planet not only has the day of the most sunlight but also the Solstice, the Sun stand-still and the gateway into transformation.

The element of Water offers emotion, imagination, intuition, and dreams - all very 'lunar' qualities. And yet June into July requires work and going outside more than ever. And so, even though we look elsewhere quite often for this, we can look to this time of the Sun moving through Cancer as a balance. Picture the water in a container and how it levels itself. Think of the water of life and how much activity there will be to maintain life.

The Sun moves through the sign of Cancer, bringing essential nurturing and nourishment and all that entails for life to continue.

Leo - July into August

Playful creator

This is generally accepted to be holiday time, playful and with memories of those 'summer' feelings. Yet the sign of Leo is the second sign to be associated with the element of Fire, and the experience will be different to that of Aries Fire (or Sagittarius Fire)! This is where we begin to see how the elements can be seemingly the same but different when applied to our beautiful signs of the zodiac.

Leo Fire energy recognises that creative energy has become material. Ruled by the Sun, there is joy as we wait for the crops to ripen in their own good time. Leo is the sign of rulers and games, fun and laughter.

I'm fond of Leo. It is my Star sign! And yet, I couldn't understand it for so long. I'm shy, and playtime at school was excruciating and yet, as a Leo, shouldn't I need to be on stage and shine? And then, I had my birth chart drawn up, and it was explained to me about the placing of signs into different areas of our lives given the time and position of my birth. It was as if a light bulb had been switched on.

As the Sun travels through the sign of Leo, it finds exactly where the Lion needs to roar. In my chart, it is in helping others go out on the stage and shine their light and roar. And I roar my message through writing, podcasts and social media.

Our Sun gives us life with regulation of warmth and light ... and rules a sign of the Zodiac after the one ruled by the Moon.

And so, as we return to our wheel of the year and Summer, this Leo energy becomes about the holidays and yet also about working in the fields to bring crops in. It also requires childlike fun outside and a fiery spirit to do whatever we are making and doing.

Virgo - August into September

Gifts & Bounty

Virgo has as its element Earth and is our second sign to be ruled by Mercury. It's absolutely fascinating to see the difference between the air sign of Gemini and the earthy Virgo, with both of them benefitting so much from the Mercurial edge!

As the Sun travels through Virgo, we are gifted so much and also have the opportunity to value our own gifts. Mercury has something to say here about times gone past and, in September, is fixated on the bounty from Nature. This is a time for:

- giving thanks for all that has been harvested
- bartering to make sure everyone had everything they needed
- Preserving and salting

Virgo is methodical in preparations because life in the darker and colder months relies on that trait. And, as Virgo equates the Hermit in Tarot, so we shine a light on the appreciation of the true wealth of caring for the self and other selves.

Libra - September into October

Watching the world slow down

Libra is the second sign associated with the element of Air and also the second sign ruled by Venus.

As the Sun reaches Libra, the world balances light and dark, and all is equal ... well, in some places, that is. Libran energy is that of the balancer, always looking to balance, and it seems so apt to have the astrological glyph of scales. It is the only astrological glyph based on an inanimate object in the whole zodiac. Venus is cool in Libra and gets to work with the autumn colours of red and gold, preparing the Earth for resting.

During this time, immediately after the Equinox and moving us through into October, we begin to go indoors and so within. We are social still but in smaller groups of neighbours and family. The nature of Libra is to choose who we have around us and where we sense the harmony. And to watch the light change as the season changes dramatically into Autumn.

Scorpio - October into November

Watching the inner self slow down

A part of the zodiac that holds the mysteries and secrets of life, love and other worlds. When the Sun moves through Scorpio, it is worthwhile taking time to ponder on the nature of your unique wisdom.

Before Pluto was discovered, the sign of Scorpio was ruled by Mars alone. And yet, by adding a joint rulership of Mars and Pluto, we can see just how much depth to the sign of Scorpio there is. Magic and action. Deep waters. Scorpio is associated with the element of Water, imagination and a subtle understanding of all things to do with the inner landscape of creativity.

As the Sun travels through Scorpio, we celebrate the mystical festival of Samhain (Halloween) and also that of All Souls Day. And there are keys to understanding Scorpio energy. The drawing together of our close friends and family, both alive and in Spirit, around the table to make plans to survive the Winter. And to grow on an inner level as the spiral of life takes us forward.

Sagittarius - November into December

Dreaming time

Where the signs are ruled by Fire, we see a push for action, and yet here we are in the darkest of months.

Sagittarius is ruled by Jupiter and is associated with the element of Fire. It took a while to unravel some of the associations with this sign; however, I particularly like that this is the sign of gambling! Life is a risk at this time of the year. Everything is drawing in with the darkness and cold weather all around. Sagittarius, as the sign of the Archer, probably makes this energy even more clear. The arrow is drawn back in the bow and carefully aimed at the centre of the target. There is nothing random about what the arrow must do. And so it is for us when we venture outside at this time. With purpose. Throwing the dice with intention of what will happen.

Jupiter is the planet of leaders and expansion. And so this is the perfect time for dreams, aims, and intentions to settle and expand. Daydream a little as there will be purpose to them!

Capricorn - December into January

Gatekeeper

The sign of Capricorn is ruled by our time-keeper planet of, Saturn. However, there is much more that goes on at this time, of course. Capricorn is of the Earth element and the keeper of the mystery of the transformation of light.

As the Sun moves into Capricorn, it stands still for the Solstice. Maybe you, like me, see this time as one of the only two true portals whereby we can raise our vibration if we choose. Saturn provides some deeply mystical knowledge, and the real alchemy of gold is to be found within this sign of the zodiac, cycles and rhythms.

This is the sunrise our ancestors waited for and the rebirth of new beginnings and knowledge. The hard work of the past months has paid off, as we are still alive and ready for the next cycle. Light begins again, and we can allow ourselves to look forward to the warmer weather. Capricorn is the sign of opening the doorway into hope ahead.

Aquarius - January into February

Becoming curious

As the Sun moves through Aquarius, it enjoys the element of Air and of being curious about what has happened outside in the world since the doors closed last October. Interestingly, the old rulership was Saturn, and so we can see that these months were still focused on work and rewards for that work, on time taking precedence, and on the deep aspects of Saturn's knowledge and understanding. However, the modern rulership of Uranus also gives a sense of the energy for new inventions and great leaps forward in technology and our 'tele' senses.

Expect social expansion tempered by boundaries of the clock or resources. Expect clearing the air and getting ready for new thoughts and ideas to be prompted by others. Delight in the absolute joy of using all the senses and feeling alive on all levels. A truly psychic sign of the zodiac.

Pisces - February into March

Dawn of a new day

And so we are at the final sign of the zodiac before the cycle begins again. The 12th sign of Pisces is of Water element and is ruled by Jupiter and also, more recently, by Neptune. The sum of the whole zodiac and the place where our Sun will travel through in order to rise through Aries and the Spring Equinox.

It is so easy to try and canter through Pisces as if on the back of a sea horse! However, this is the sign of the zodiac where we see our energetic Aries pioneering spirit gathering all of the gifts together from throughout the whole year to prepare for the next level of life. All of the senses are activated, and all of the seeds are sown, grown, digested and matured. As the Sun moves through Pisces, we can take the time to emerge out into the light and the world above!

***We all have all of the signs of the zodiac
in our birth charts.***

.

festivals & 'ho' to the sun

There are other festivals of celebration at this time, and all will be honouring the beginning of harvest. It's a time for village fetes and fun runs. And, in earlier times, we have records of village walks taking place with music and food to make the day a joyous one.

Schools are closed for the month of August, and factories would have a two-week break at this time. All with the deeper acknowledgment that every single person was required to work in the fields bringing the crops in.

Wales holds the National Eisteddfod usually in August, and the location alternates yearly between North and South Wales. It's a celebration of the arts and especially of poetry spoken in the Welsh language. There are awards given, and the whole event is shrouded in mystery and ritual led by Druids and keeping true to the wonderful, vibrant history of the Nation.

Look out for village and town 'days' of celebration as their roots often hold a rich tradition for the area.

notes from the ancestors

My Dad was born in Devon and, even though he chose to join the army, came from a sea-faring family. I find it interesting that he married my Mum, who also came from a family reliant on the sea. Her father, my Grandad Ted, grew up in a fishing port, and everything around the town had either to do with the sea or the church, as was my Dad's.

The sea connects land with other land and helps regulate our climate.

Without clouds forming over the sea, our rainfall would be dramatically reduced.

It's a strange thing, the pull of the sea.

I feel it keenly at times.

There is a word in the Welsh language, 'hiraeth', which doesn't directly translate into another language. As far as I can delve into it, it is about a calling of home. Hiraeth is a feeling of nostalgia for the mountains and valleys of Wales. It's a pull of the heart and the emotions for something deeper than words, such as connection, home-sickness, love of the land, the joy of being with family, sadness of something lost, beauty of landscape ...

When dowsing, there is a pull through my body from deep within the earth. If we accept that our earth is a living and breathing entity, then can we also accept that she has a language and emotions that we are a part of?

Even a short walk into a forest very quickly transforms the atmosphere around us into a different type of silence and a sense of ancient history all around.

We know that trees have connections with each other through their roots as well as their branches and leaves. They form an incredibly important part of our own ability to live on Earth by giving us oxygen, removing carob-dioxide, providing living spaces for wildlife, and, it's now being proven scientifically, talk to each other through their root systems to warn of catastrophes and maybe to celebrate too.

As we are now into the second half of our year, and the time of the light becoming less, we look further back to our ancestors. To the time when we relied on the earth much more than even my grandad did. Grandad Ted grew fruit and vegetables through the war to feed the hospital and continued even after he retired. He was completely in tune with the rhythm of nature and her seasons - he couldn't have achieved what he did if not!

But we need to go back further to the times when there were no buses or cars, when all there was came from the Earth in the small area around where we lived. And then to think about how we kept the cycle of life going.

The corn dolly is storing seeds for the next year.

Do we still have the knowledge of what could be grown in the same field year after year and what couldn't, and so where the practise of rotation of crops is necessary?

Go back further and listen to the air to understand the weather, sensing where animals were for either hunting or danger, learning from elders which berries were nutritional and which were poisonous.

Our ancestors have so much to tell us, and it is becoming more and more crucial that we hear them. The trees with their root systems are warning of the loss of great chunks of living land and seas. Give and take has become out of balance ... that's if it ever was balanced to start with. Our ancestors ate, drank and used what they needed to survive and to grow—and returned their natural waste to the earth.

The more I connect in and ask the ancestors for information, the more I have come to understand that 'balance' wasn't in operation. It didn't exist as a word or a notion.

Our ancestors knew that, in order to keep living and growing, there had to be a relationship between them and nature that had nothing to do with give and take. It was about living alongside each other, connected as beings, joined as if one - ensuring that every part of the 'whole' would be able to move into the next season and then the next.

And, because Grandad Ted taught me so much, I have to tell you about his compost heap. It was beautiful. He had a fence around it and treated it with as much love and joy as his best vegetables or the flowers he grew for my Nan. Everything went into the compost heap from the kitchen, and it gave a richness of nutrients to the soil. But not for the following year. I cannot remember now how many years he would leave the compost to rot down before using it. Although use it, eventually, he did.

being

To make a corn dolly, the straws of corn or wheat are soaked in water to dampen them, and this can take a while - anything from a half hour to overnight. Then, the straw will be malleable enough to be able to bend it into the shapes required for the dolly without breaking the stems and tied with ribbons.

Crop circles are formed by the stems of wheat still growing in the fields and being bent over to form circles and patterns. They are not broken. And there is the puzzle - how to perfectly bend the stems without breaking any of them and form the intricate patterns that we see.

Try it! Dry some grasses, or buy some stems of wheat or corn, and dampen them to make them supple and then make a dolly or a pattern.

And, if you're pulling them up from the ground, always ask permission from the plant before and be open to a 'not today'. Plants know their purpose in their lives, and it may be to help us understand something better, or it may be to remain where they are! The seeds decide to grow and live out their purpose - how magical is that!

doing

It's time for some clearing and making certain that we tread lightly on this amazing blue planet of ours. As we explore and attune ourselves to the earth, we become better stewards of the planet. We are able to appreciate the incredible ecosystem from both the minute through to the great expanses which enable us to live and grow.

It's time to give back actively and take time out to remove rubbish and litter pick an area close to home.

It's time to accentuate some amazing growth and show our patch of home turf some 'Venus goddess of abundance' love. Perhaps plant some more seeds for next year or leave a beautifully painted stone for somebody to find and be joyful about. I'll leave it to you to know instinctively what your part of the planet would love to receive!

playing

Schools are out for Summer, and mostly the children still break for holidays of six weeks or more. This is left over from the time when everyone in a town or a village needed to work to bring the harvest in. Often, this origin of the long school break is lost; however, when you think about it, it was logical to need all hands out in the fields to harvest and preserve enough provisions to last through the Winter!

School is out, and you have that feeling of joyous expansion of days filled with ... well, what?!

What did you love to do in those first days of the Summer holidays when the weeks stretched ahead and September seemed a long way in the distance? We're of the generations where harvesting doesn't fall into Summers for many of us, but we can still find 'pick your own' fields for strawberries or gooseberries.

Maybe you'll go for bike rides or bus trips. Or the cinema to watch a fun-filled film. Perhaps to play a record and spend a whole afternoon listening to music.

Take back to those feelings of 'schools out' and do something the younger you would have done. Somehow, I suspect, it is likely to be something outdoors!

stillness

And time to consider the crucial importance of intentional space between.

During a writing course, I think it was for radio screen-plays, the tutor mentioned the power of silence and the space between dialogue. I've worked with this concept ever since as it gives the listener, our inner self, a pause to absorb what has been said, and it also gives a weight to the emotional sense being accessed.

If we consider our emotion as being an extra sense of perception, then it follows that, in certain circumstances, emotion may need more time to tell us the message of experience. Earlier in this chapter, we thought about the connections formed between the roots of trees, and we have no real idea if this is through the roots actually touching or whether they are able to converse via the space between the roots.

We have a space between paragraphs in writing and put space around pictures and photographs in frames. There are spaces in music for the notes to end before the next one begins. I'm sure when you think about this, you'll find other ways that spaces are given and made in order to allow emotion, thought, colour and weight to apply.

Space offers a place or position for something else to occur … or maybe not to occur! Intentional space definitely does as it is placed by the artist, craftsperson, writer, or singer in order for the listener or viewer to have that space. The space we create when clearing is different as, mostly, we are making way for something not quite known to enter.

Sit still and wonder at the spaces.

Even the birds sing their songs

with spaces between.

dear friend

Dear friend,

We're beginning to withdraw and yet to also be outside harvesting. I wonder how you found the space for being in your 'school out' energy? Did you play loud music from an LP or go strawberry picking, which is how I remember my own 'school out'? Have you noticed any crop circles in local news and wondered whether there are 'extraterrestrial' beings working to provide them for us? And, if so, for what purpose?

Before we move gracefully into the next turn of the wheel of the year, I invite you to flick back through the pages of the last chapter and note which ideas, thoughts, stories, practises and celebrations resonated.

As we move into this first harvest time and, now, onward into the real harvest of Autumn, it is with joy in our hearts to see what has been created all around us and our part in this. By completing some form of clearing of space, we offer more to come ...

As always, with love from Alison x

autumn

Winter Solstice /
Yule

Halloween/
Samhain

Imbolc

Autumn Equinox /
Harvest

Spring Equinox /
Ostara

Lammas /
Harvest

Beltane /
May Day

Summer Solstice /
Midsummer

autumn - september & october

As the sun moves into the zodiac sign of Libra, with equal light and dark, we celebrate the festival of Autumn Equinox and the real deep autumnal months. This heralds the season of recognising gifts of the bounty from nature that will nourish and sustain us through Winter.

Take, for one example, textiles and producing warm clothing and bedding. Whether we are using the wool from sheep or a fibre crop such as flax, there are whole processes to go through before our raw material resembles something useful for us. It takes time creating textiles from either what we have grown in the earth or waiting for the animals to grow their fleece ready for shearing and then to be used.

I've learned a little bit about spinning, carding and the process of how we obtain the wool or yarn to knit and weave textiles with. It's an intricate process, and I think that's an important note to acknowledge as we go into this Autumnal season, which begins with Lammas and reaches intensity at Autumn Equinox and beyond.

The day and night of Autumn Equinox are both similar and yet also very different to the Spring Equinox we celebrated in March - because now is when we start to see what we've made, what we've created, what we've got, what we've stored and just what we're made of!

And as always, we begin with finding our centre and our balance ...

grounding & connecting

Take a moment to sense where you are by standing (or sitting) still and reach your awareness down through your tailbone to the ground beneath and then further down until you sense the centre of the Earth.

Connect to the Earth.

And then expand your awareness out to the sky above your head and the infinity of the universe and space.

Connected to the Earth and the Universe.

Tuning your frequency into the Earth and the Universe.

And then feel the horizon of our planet stretching out from either side of you and in front and behind and all around you.

Your light shines out to all the compass points.

All is in balance, and as you are at one with the earth, you feel strong in all directions.

Reinforce your bubble of light all around you and know that you are at one with your body and the body of the earth and universe.

Raise your hands up to the sky and then slowly take them down to touch the earth.

Stand up straight and tall, and be proud of the wonderful human you are.

And now you are grounded, tuned in to your own connected frequency of the Universe itself and ready to celebrate this time of balance during both the light of day and the resting time of night!!

autumn equinox

The Autumn Equinox with the Sun moving into the sign of Libra is the time of equal light and dark - the same number of hours of daylight and nighttime.

The Equinox sets the scene for the coming weeks until our next festival of Samhain (Halloween) at the end of October. It also sets the scene for the next six months, and for this, we need to look back to Spring Equinox and the legends surrounding Demeter and her daughter Persephone.

Stories vary, although there is a central theme in the tale of Persephone. The contract made between Demeter and Hades requires he has Persephone by his side for half of the year. And so the Autumn Equinox dawns, and, with light and dark balanced as it were, Persephone must leave her mother above the earth and travel down into the darkness of the labyrinth to join her husband. Her Mother gives her a golden thread to guide her back when the wheel of the year will turn again towards Spring. However, for the next six months, Demeter will grieve for her daughter, and the land falls dark and silent.

For us, we can take the story and use the symbolism to give our bodies, as well as the earth, time for resting and recharging. It is time to appreciate our gifts and nature. Time to plan, muse and dream.

Our ancestors had another reason to celebrate this festival, and that was to welcome the harvest and all that would sustain them through the Winter. Little will be grown in the months ahead, and so what is in the barns, pantries, and outhouses had to be enough.

Libra is the zodiac sign of balance or, more to the point, of looking for and gaining balance. The Spring Equinox was full of the potential of creativity and production, with all of the emphasis on growing. And, now we're at the other side of that energy, Autumn Equinox, and time for harvesting, collecting, and storing.

Moving on through September and October, we will see creativity beginning to go under the surface and be hidden. It's a very mystical time and the time of sacred loss beautifully expressed within the Demeter and Persephone story. This is where we see a shift of light into dark, the outer into the inner and the resting time.

But nothing, especially in nature, is ever just resting or 'not doing' anything. Demeter and 'mother energy' above the ground. Persephone and 'daughter energy' beneath the ground. Both allowing time to rest and make plans for where our land wants to grow and where we plant and grow crops for next year. We can't possibly grow things in the same place continually as it would exhaust the ground, and so there has to be crop rotation and resting or fallow time. The same is true for us, too, as we need this time of retreat as much as we need the spring and the high summer.

cleansing, bounty & gifts

Part of our preparations for this season of Autumn is to think about organising, cleansing, tidying and getting ready to store our provisions for the coming months. Just as the squirrels store their food beneath the surface of the earth, we have an innate need to ensure we have enough. The cleaning and tidying have a different feel in this season. In springtime, we throw open the windows and brush away the winter cobwebs. In Autumn, we are readying ourselves and our homes for living through colder months and storing inside what we will need to see us through.

Consider the ground outside, the earth of our fields and our gardens. What grew this year, and what didn't grow? Sometimes, what didn't grow or manifest has more for us to ponder on than what did. Our gifts from this year of growth may vary from what our original intentions and aspirations were as we adjusted and accommodated changing circumstances or new ideas. There will also be those gifts which take longer than a year to come to fruition. As always, and taking our cues from Nature, a fruit tree planted may take several years to properly bear fruit, whereas a flower achieved its potential this year, perhaps.

Traditional Harvest festivals will have tables brimming with produce of all types. Fruit, bread, vegetables and more are all gathered together and celebrated as the bounty from nature for the year.

We have also grown and brought potentials into the world this year. By celebrating and appreciating our own gifts, we all feel the ripple of bountiful energy emanating around the world. The joy of the time of balance is that the Northern hemisphere will be celebrating the harvest in September and October, whilst the Southern hemisphere will gather their gifts together in March & April Like a wave of appreciation echoing around our globe as each part of the world sees some form of a seasonal change.

As the seasons change, nature grows, rests and then grows again, as do we. We age. Animals and birds have life spans. Everything moves forward on our planet and in our universe.

As an astrologer, I have spent so much time dispelling the myths of planets going backwards. They don't! Nothing in our Universe travels backwards … at least nothing we know of.

When we refer to retrograde motions of planetary bodies, it is that their movement has altered and, from our perception here on Earth, appears to be going into reverse. The energy changes as the relationship between ourselves on Earth and the particular planet has altered. Indeed, the pattern made of energy will be different in a subtle way. This retrograde motion and the resulting change in frequency offers a respite from the energy of direct and is best described as a pause with meaning.

And to conquer the biggest myth of all ... 'Mercury in Retrograde' will NOT make our washing machines break down or cause technical glitches to happen. A change in Mercury energy offers us opportunities to pause and reflect and then make our systems run better or even to rewrite and correct chapters in a book. It is useful to know when these great energies are available for us to use and to choose to use very effectively!

Energy from planetary bodies is just that.

Energy.

We get to choose what we do with it!

festivals & 'ho' to the sun

I've already mentioned harvest festivals, and whether you go to an organised one or, perhaps, sit outside to celebrate the harvest, there is an energy to celebrating what has been produced, which you will find all over the world in different cultures.

September is the first month to have an 'r' in the name since April, and there are quiet rules around this to do with fish. Only eating shellfish when there is no 'r' in the month comes to mind. I was brought up in the East of England, UK, and Cromer crabs would, traditionally, only be available May through August. And yet, oysters are in season from September! I suspect these quiet 'rules' allowed for fishing to remain sustainable.

You may be familiar with the song 'Widecombe Fair' and be interested that there is an annual fair in Dartmoor, England, in the village named in the song! Usually held around the second week in September, it celebrates the produce of the area. I dowsed many stone circles in the area years ago, and the energies are, I can only really describe, of dancing. The fairly nearby village of Tintagel is also well worth a visit with its history steeped in Arthurian Legend ...

As it is also a time for making jams from fruit, cider from apples and other preserves, you may find farms offering produce fairs and even bags of windfall apples at the sides of the roads.

using your birth chart

The birth charts commonly used by us now are circular, which makes so much sense in the world for us. In medieval times, astrology charts were set up in a rectangle, which, perhaps, relates to the worldview of then. However, by using a circle inside a circle, it is easier to visualise the Universe as operating around Earth - making it easier for our understanding and interpreting the planetary energies.

If you have access to your chart or even to a chart of a moment in time, please look at it and visualise yourself standing in the centre circle. To the left and the right is the horizon. And so another way of working with this energy, this Equinox energy, and beginning to think about what we're going to be doing in these darker months is to look at what's above the horizon in your chart and what's beneath the horizon.

This is, perhaps, a different way of looking at a birth chart and a really good way to begin to understand parts of your chart that maybe you don't display, necessarily, because it's beneath the horizon. Without looking deeper at the individual houses, for instance, just give yourself permission to have a look at what's under the surface.

What's beneath that horizon?

What planets and stars were on the other side of the world being visible when you were born?

Maybe that will open another door by seeing what is above and what is below in your chart.

At every moment in time, the planets are making different patterns of energy and will never return to the same design. It is what makes our charted moments in time so unique. Our Earth is moving through space, and the planetary bodies we watch are also moving, and all are using different orbits. Using our birth chart as an example and a really good measure of just how the patterns of energy change, we can apply where the stars are right now to our chart and look at the influences available in the pattern on top of the positions of the stars at our birth. In astrology, this offers us opportunities and potentials to see where great choices are offered and new directions to be taken.

*All by our choice. Nothing is fated.
As human beings, we have free will
and free choice unless restricted by
other human beings, of course.*

*Watching the impact of the stars on our own personal astrology
gives us more information about ourselves and our movement
forward through life.*

Stars, planets & an asteroid

So what about those planetary bodies and the patterns
they make? If we were to plot where Uranus, our planet of
electrifying change, is right now, then we know, due to his orbit,
that he will take approximately 84 years to return to the same
position in the sky after having visited every sign of the zodiac
on his travels. An interesting note here is that when I first
began my professional life as an astrologer, a Uranus return was
barely noted. However, now there are more and more people
in their mid-eighties making life-changing decisions to move
house or even begin to study.

So what about the other planets and their orbits making
patterns with us and each other? Each star, planet and asteroid
that we use commonly within astrology will have its own orbit
and, within that time period, visit each constellation/sign of
the zodiac in turn. By using a good ephemeris, we can plot
where the planetary bodies are at any given moment in time
and then work out the relationships that they make with each

other and with us on Earth. Each pattern of planetary energies is completely unique, never to be seen again, and that is what makes our birth charts completely individual!

Stars, planets & an asteroid in order!

Sun

Mercury

Venus

Earth (and we have our own Moon)

Mars

Jupiter

Saturn

Chiron

Uranus

Neptune

Pluto

The Sun ☉

Our star of Creativity, showing us character and expression, the Sun, will take around 365.3 days to return to the same position in the sky as from the moment of plotting where he is. In Western astrology, we tend to always know where the Sun was at our birth, and so this is usually known as our star sign. The Sun rules the sign of Leo and thus can bring leadership to his role wherever he is in the sky!

We refer to the Sun as masculine energy; however, it can also be referred to as feminine. Indeed, our ancestors (and some modern viewpoints) saw the Moon as masculine. By giving the planets a gender, we are, perhaps, diminishing their energy, although so much of our understanding of those energies actually comes from Celtic, Greek & Roman mythology. I suspect we need to look deeper at the mythological stories about the gods and goddesses to truly understand this phenomenon. To say that they are all bigger, wider, deeper and more full of energy than we can possibly really process may get close to why we offer genders, colours, stories and expressions of power to each of them.

Mercury ☿ and Venus ♀

These two planets are between us and the Sun, closer to the Sun than we are. And so their orbits are such that they will visit all of the signs of the zodiac and then begin again during one of our calendar years!

Mercury, ruler of Gemini and Virgo, has an 88-day orbit and brings energy of thoughts, curiosity and different languages. In mythology, he was known as the messenger planet and took communications from Earth to the gods and vice versa.

Venus has a 225-day orbit and brings energy of beauty, abundance and crops. I've mentioned elsewhere that Venus rules both Taurus and Libra, and so has knowledge of both growth and harvest.

The Moon ☾

Our beautiful Moon, with her stunningly available goddess energy of intuition, imagination & emotional depth of understanding, will take around 27.3 nights to orbit around us. She rules the sign of Cancer and, remembering that we have all of the signs of the zodiac in our birth charts, where she is can bring a sense of how you feel at home with yourself.

Mars ♂

Mars is our first planet to be on the other side of us and the Sun, and so he takes around 687 days in his orbit, giving us almost two years before he has completed the journey through all of the constellations and returning to begin again. He is seen as a tremendous active energy, rules Aries after all, and ignites passion and projects! It is a relatively fast energy of inspiration, and, of course, he is known as the 'red' planet.

Jupiter ♃

Jupiter is the planet for spirituality, expansion & wealth in the true sense of the word. His orbit through the constellations is around 12 years, and so we have time to use his energy in understanding our pathways forward, for example. There is a royal sense to this energy, and often, the colour associated will be purple. As the ruler of Sagittarius, this planet shows us a bigger perspective or wider point of view.

Saturn ♄

I'm an astrologer who doesn't believe in time - yes, I opened this book with that! And yet, I love our timekeeping planet of Saturn. Having Saturn make a particular aspect to our charts can offer the type of change that requires fortitude and strength and yet offers us rewards afterwards that we cannot even guess at the time! Saturn, during his 28/29-year cycle, brings rewards, challenges, and opportunities to tend to minute parts of a process and to understand how time works for each of us as individuals. Phew. Yes. He is an amazing planetary energy to work with and helps us all learn languages, crafts, technology and whatever we are called to! He rules the sign of Capricorn, which we meet at the December Solstice, and so is the energy behind opening the gateway of transformation - a deeply magical planet.

Uranus ♅

I mentioned Uranus with his 84-year cycle and as the planet of electrifying changes. He also brings in epiphanies and sudden inspirations to make big alterations to our lives. Uranus was the first planet in 1781 to be 'seen' through a telescope, which, in itself, is something to marvel at.

Aquarius has Saturn as the old/traditional ruler and now includes Uranus as a more modern ruler.

Neptune ♆ and Puto ♇

Neptune takes around 165 years in its planetary orbit around the zodiac, and Pluto 248 years. It is unlikely that in our lifetimes, we will see either of these planets return to the same point in our birth charts as at our birth! Neptune - Visionary, ingenuity, and deep imagination. Pluto - into even deeper waters of soul intuition. Both are transformational, magical and powerful for our life journeys and whilst we really do get to choose whether we use them or not, their abilities to bring change can be spectacular.

Neptune rules Pisces together with Jupiter, and we can see how those two planets ruling this sign can bring a visionary intensity to imagination.

Pluto rules Scorpio together with Mars and benefits from both planets in its associations with, delving deep into, for instance, our values.

Chiron ⚷

I'm including the asteroid Chiron as I've found, over many years, that the orbit of 50 years has much to offer for soul journey information at its return. I have devoted years of research to Chiron and his devotion to the journey of the Hero/Heroine, especially for uncovering not only what we may need to pay attention to but also where we can help others. With a 50-year cycle, there is, perhaps, the root of the saying 'Life begins at 50' (I know - I've borrowed this from our 40s, but it really does fit so much more!).

And so …

Just for a few moments, picture these stars all moving to their own dance and creating ripples of energy between them as they move near to each other and then away. All are weaving together to tell their stories … and because we are based on Earth, we are at the centre of this dancing pulse of the universe …

notes from the ancestors

I know very little about my Nan on my mother's side other than what has already been written in this book. I spent so much time living with her and Grandad Ted and yet remember few conversations. She was very small and barely as tall as my Grandad's shoulders. What I do remember is that she was always doing something, and mostly that was in the kitchen.

To make blackcurrant jelly, she would suspend muslin between the backs of two kitchen chairs with the bowl underneath to catch the strained juices. I spent hours holding skeins of wool for her to wind into balls for knitting cardigans and jumpers. She made marmalades and chutneys and stored vegetables for the Winter. My Nan, just like yours, no doubt, was of the time before freezers and when fridges were a new invention and something still so special.

After Grandad Ted retired and they moved to the next village, she went to work in a care home for older people. It was quite a walk from her new house, but she said it was her way of being useful and of being with people. I guess she felt quite lonely, having lived in the cottages near to the hospital all of her married life. I can still picture her walking down the road with a small black shopping bag, sometimes catching the bus but mostly walking, and I went with her a few times. It was a happy place filled with laughter, and she loved working there. Looking back on those times now, I feel they were a major part of how, when I found myself working in a hospice, it was easy for me to relate to the patients as it was so like the home I visited with Nan.

I am trained in massage and in Reiki to Master level and worked for a while in a group of hospices as a complementary therapist. Hospices are often overlooked as far as funding is concerned and rely on donations and a large volunteer workforce. My work was funded, which showed the emphasis given to holistic care for end of life. I loved working there, and wherever I was based, whether with in-patients or day patients, it was always an incredibly positive energy to be around.

I'm also so lucky to have met so many magical people who work tirelessly with the elderly as well as with people at the end of life. For example, my English school teacher became a great friend of mine for many years after I left school. Joyce R. retired the year I left school and then volunteered at a hospital for so many years she was awarded a long service medal.

And then, as if being in her 80s was another beginning, she went to visit the elderly living around her neighbourhood. They were younger than her, it has to be said!

Back to my story of Nan and her role in my book, though.

Sitting and talking to our ancestors can offer surprising notions and feelings that they want to convey. I asked Nan what she would like to offer to you through this book, and this was one of our conversations.

"Thank you, Nan, for taking care of me all those Summers."

"We had fun, didn't we, Alison? You were a serious child and quiet, but Grandad said you heard more than we all knew."

"I loved being with you and sleeping in the big bed with blankets and an eiderdown."

I'm going to add a note here that this was a memory I'd forgotten but realised afterwards that the weight of the blankets and bedding had made me feel so safe and secure enough to sleep deeply.

"I remember the silence from outside and just how dark it was - so different to at home where there always seemed to be lights outside at night."

"Alison, you were always too thin. I never could get enough meat on your bones, but I tried. And you were too quiet. You were scared of your own shadow, and there was nothing Grandad and I could do about that."

"Nan, this makes me sad. I knew you loved me and didn't know how much you saw."

"We loved you and saw you. That is what was, is, needed. To see people."

"Thank you, Nan and I love you."

Those three words of 'To See People' are now at the heart of everything I do, offer, and am about. And I expand it to:

To See People;
To See Nature;
To See the Universe;
And to knit it all together and
really live inside life itself.

being

There is a golden thread for all of us, whether reaching backwards through time to the ancestors of our ancestors or forward and into our next chapters. I'd invite you to take some thread and, if possible, golden. Weave it into a bracelet for yourself.

This is Autumn energy and, to go back to the beginning of this chapter:

"Now is when we really start to see what we've made, what we've created, what we've got, what we've stored and just what we're made of!"

Weave your recollections of the past six months into your creation and make this a part of the celebration for moving into the deeper waters yet to come.

doing

Nature, Earth, teaches us so much, and as we listen to her message of the bounty, there's a beauty in how Autumn changes the colours and hues all around us.

We will explore more about rituals and observances in our next chapter; however, this is a great time to begin to think about what signs, symbols, and correspondences have to help our brains hear those messages.

I'm going to put my practical hat on here and say that we must always remember that sometimes an apple is just an apple and has no deeper meaning than something nourishing to eat. And yet, if we slice an apple in half, we see a pentagram, a magical symbol, with a middle made up of the pips/seeds. We wouldn't eat the apple core, and yet it either rots down to become food compost, or the birds will eat it. We all know the fable of

William Tell and his ability to shoot an arrow from a crossbow through an apple placed on his son's head. It is a part of the legend of freedom from oppression. And then Isaac Newton is said to have determined the nature of gravity by watching apples fall. So our apple, whilst being 'just' an apple, also represents magic, freedom, and understanding.

Correspondences - something that represents something else.

Venus has, at heart, the growing and abundance of energy. Ruling both Taurus and Libra (apt for our Autumnal celebrations!) She loves all produce, from the production of it through to the harvest and usefulness of it. Venus is all about celebrating the abundance of the planets, of the Earth and of what's been produced. Venus's colours are green and also the pink of love.

Think of something that represents a celebration of what you've done, what you've achieved, and what's happened since Spring.

And also, ponder a little bit on how much energy went into the intentions you set in the Spring.

Traditional correspondences for Venus energy are fruit, nuts, golden colour, red and leaves - autumn leaves are incredibly beautiful and not all the same colour.

.

Could you collect a fallen leaf and bring it into your celebrations?

And a nut to represent the seeds we take forward?

playing

Is there still a warm evening when you can go outside and dance? Is it a joyful time of collecting berries and nuts from hedgerows and gardens?

As the days shorten and the children return to school, there is time to begin new timetables and remember old routines. Set new structures in place and begin the processes required of us to begin the next school term or chapter of the book.

What will you do over the next few weeks to remember how to play in the Sun?

It's important we remember how to play.

As well as how to be still.

stillness

This is our time of balance, and we began this season with the Autumn Equinox of equal light and dark. We go through September and October, moving towards our next season. And yet the purpose of these 'Stillness' sections is to allow us to rest inside each moment, and this Autumn season is all about going into the 'resting time' and the 'dreaming time'.

As we walk outside now, we see the green disappearing and our land withdrawing into itself. There are empty spaces where once there were crops and composting materials where once there were vegetables growing. However, those 'empty' spaces are not devoid of life - they are becoming different and an altered energy. Our earth has given so much of crops, fruit, nuts and vegetables and is now withdrawing and taking what it needs to beneath the surface.

It's time for rest and for us to be alongside the earth as she withdraws to recharge herself.

If we look at our birth charts again, there will likely be parts unoccupied by stars, and we will call them empty houses or areas. However, they are not actually devoid of energy because every part of our birth chart has the energy of a sign of the zodiac.

That part of our birth chart, with no planet or star inside, has the purest energy from that sign of the zodiac.

And, at this time of withdrawal of Earth into herself, so we can see Earth as retreating into the purest form of her.

Go outside, if it is warm and safe for you to do so, and just allow your imagination to witness our Earth in her purest of forms.

And rest a while.

dear friend

Dear friend,

Balance. This is another season where we are watching the balancing actions of nature turn and turn around. Did you find something to celebrate that you've done this year? Seeds planted in February and March will have grown and matured ... or maybe not. It's perfectly fine in this lifetime of ours to experiment with our gifts and talents and see what works and moves with us and what doesn't. Remember that nothing is ever lost, wasted or of no purpose. Everything has purpose and may just not be as we expect it to be. The magic of life!

Before we move slowly and gently into the next turn of the wheel of the year, I invite you to flick back through the pages of the last chapter and note which ideas, thoughts, stories, practises and celebrations resonated.

Expanding on the words of my Nan seems appropriate here as I walk by your side:

To See People;
To See Nature;
To See the Universe;
And to knit it all together and really live inside life itself.

As always, with love from Alison x

a moment out of time

Dear Friend

There came a point while writing this book for you that I realised I was lost. I couldn't find my way forward. The strange thing is that this book has a structure and a calendar to it. It's own calendar of a rhythm and a pulse from the natural turning of the Earth and her seasons.

Winter into Spring. Spring into Summer. Summer into Autumn. Autumn into Winter. And the cross-quarter festivals which bring us a gentle nudge from season into season so that everything runs perfectly and, dare I say, like clockwork!

And yet.

Here I am. Wondering how to go from one season into another. Feeling like Persephone may sometimes feel. Even though she has her golden thread connecting her with the depths of the labyrinth and the outside world ... even as we know that there is only one way to walk ... even with, as we know, time moves onwards and forwards ...

Because time does move forward, or rather, we move forward within time as we know it. In another chapter, we talk about the universe, our home, only able to move onwards in patterns of energy. And we age with time, too - like fine wine maturing. So, all things move forward.

This chapter will move us on - me and you.

But *differently*.

the ancients

We know of incredibly advanced civilisations that have existed. By studying artefacts, excavations of buildings and even cities, historical documentary evidence gives us access to see how our ancient ancestors not only lived their lives but gathered their own information. The Egyptians have probably left us the most recorded texts through hieroglyphics, but we can also gain much from cave paintings and drawings through to the way that the Mayans constructed their temples.

And so, let's think about the Mayans again for a moment.

The Mayans, in their measurement of time, discovered that every four years, they needed to add an extra day - just like our leap year.

The planets and stars do not conform to any regularity, and so will never allow us to construct a calendar which is correct by the Sun! There will always be some form of adjustment made.

And so the Mayans introduced their extra day (thought to be mid-July) and called it a day out of time. What a beautiful way of expressing this time adjustment, and this is something we can use.

So if you were to take a moment, a moment with no measurement, a moment is whatever it is, as long or as short.

Take a moment out of time.

What is your passion? What beats your heart? What do you love to do?

And why not? Take a moment to do that.

Have a moment out of time or a day out of time.

And enjoy.

Life doesn't have to be all about routine and what we should do when we should do it.

Take a moment with no expectations. Use the time for self-care, soul nourishment, loving, being with people, spontaneously having a picnic ...

Take that moment out of time and enjoy.

And, maybe, pay homage to the Mayans and drink chocolate! The Mayans used the cacao bean as currency, and their nobility drank a frothy drink made from it. Cacao was a super important part of ancient Mayan culture with many different uses. However, for us and our own moments out of time, perhaps it forms a part of celebrating that we, as humanity, are still around!

Or just add in something that you love to use as a part of celebrating a moment of 'you' time.

Heart

Our beating hearts keep the blood circulating and our life force moving. Emotions are felt in the heart, and when we say, 'Let's get to the heart of the matter', we are really talking about the deepest and most truthful part of whatever we're analysing.

Hearts in the playing card decks become the suit of Cups in Tarot, which is worth pondering. A cup is empty, full, and runs over. And yet, when the heart is in pain, it can feel as if a sword has been used. The Fire element from the Swords suit and the water element from Cups don't really seem to mix. And yet, let's ponder on love for a moment. There is the seemingly randomness of falling in love and the speed at which it can happen, and also the slow building of love that takes time.

When we are born, it is under a unique map of the stars which will never be seen again. That snapshot of the universe forms our birth chart or star map and, using it brings us to our sense of who we are and to our own beating hearts.

Touching the Earth and spending time watching seeds grow into plants shows us the strength, and sometimes fragility, of life.

> *Our Earth has a heartbeat all of her own,*
> *and when we take the time to listen,*
> *speaks a language of beauty and love*
> *and of survival.*

The Coffee Cup

An alternative subtitle for this book was going to be 'When recycling a coffee cup just isn't enough,' and I still have that in mind as I write.

We already recycle, reduce and reuse as much as we can, but what happens next? I was struck by the whole 'journey' our recyclable coffee cup could possibly take. It will be washed in hot water, put in some form of container, collected by a van, driven to somewhere to be sorted and then taken to somewhere else to be made into something else. Or it will be buried in the earth.

How many times can something be recycled?

And here's a thought for the philosophical discussions around our chapter of going from lost to finding our way - are we recycling ourselves or evolving into new?

the great age of aquarius

Astrologically, a Great Age is considered around 2,000 years, and the cycle through the 12 signs of the zodiac is around 24,000 years. So this is 'big history', and here is just one way of looking at it!

Whenever the subject of cusps arises, and whether there can be such a thing as 'between' zodiac signs, I will always say 'No'. A planet (or star) is always in one sign of the zodiac or another - and I do often repeat that!

But we have to consider these great ages of 2,000 years plus for each sign of the zodiac as the exception to the rule. Moving from one Great Age into the next has been, if we look back through history, not something to be pinned down to an exact moment in time, and so we can allow the thought of there being a cusp.

Even as I'm writing this, there are arguments all around as to whether we have left the Age of Pisces and arrived in the Age of Aquarius.

By the way, a Great Year is based on the Equinox pointers to constellations and moves the opposite way to how our planet, the stars, and our universe perform. The astronomy of the Precession of the Vernal Equinoxes is complex and would require a book of its own to fully explain! And so, where we would expect the next sign of the zodiac from Pisces to be Aries (our personal astrology), it becomes Aquarius (Great Year astrology!).

Astronomers as far back in time as Ancient Egypt concluded that our planet Earth's movement in relation to the constellations had this greater cosmic cycle, and although we really cannot say the exact time that we will enter The Age of Aquarius, I do believe we are there!

My own deliberations on this new Great Age are that it won't actually be about technology as our reliance on tech seems to have become the same as a reliance on religion or even on retail, and it belongs firmly in the times we are moving on from.

Left to their own devices, there is no sign more joyously perceptive and visionary than that of Pisces, and, as we all have access to that energy in different ways, it truly is a wonderful part of our birth charts to explore.

And yet, globally, we can also see the beautiful Pisces energies of using psychic abilities, inspirational imagination and empathy have been dampened down (or maybe had to be) with the injection of organised religion, the industrial revolution and the rapid growth of the computer game realm!

And so my thoughts are that, as we move into this new Age, we will be slowly unwrapping the wonderful energy to take forward with us from the Age of Pisces. This includes listening to our own unique inner voices and creativity inspired by the imagination. And, given the air element associated with Aquarius, together with the sense of world curiosity, there is a need to extend and expand our own abilities to encompass each other. True telepathy will only be available through love for each other and with good intentions. That's just for starters, as we connect with each other in ways not even in our consciousness as yet.

I really believe we ARE in The Great Age of Aquarius and that we have approximately 2,000 years to shift humanity into a very different collective consciousness with what we have learned from the Age of Pisces.

What do you think?

rituals

Our day-to-day lives are punctuated by rituals. The obvious ones are birthdays, weddings, religious festivals, funerals, and special parties. There are the festivals that we are observing detailed in this book, too.

A ritual act or actions allow us to take a moment to be still and with a purpose. It invites us to consider what we are celebrating, processing or watching. There is, whether we acknowledge it or not, a sacredness to a ritual. Think of the birthday cake with candles denoting the birthday reached and being placed in the centre of the table. Lights are dimmed as the candles are lit, and the birthday person blows out the candles and makes a wish. The only time it is said (!) that candles should be blown out rather than extinguished. A birthday wish is sent out into the universe by the act of blowing air. An intention is set in place.

Magic is invited.

A ritual can, then, be as simple as based around blowing the candles out on a birthday cake through to more complicated ones that take days of a certain practice enacted every day.

If we consider that a ritual is something that suspends our normal activity and allows time for consideration of a different way of being (the birthday wish, perhaps), then the significance of allowing time for special moments in time becomes apparent.

notes from the ancestors

We visited Nan and Grandad Ted occasionally on Sundays when my brother and I were growing up. This was when they lived in their new home, and it was an occasion to go for tea. We always sat at the table, quite formally, I remember, which was different to when I stayed with them, and we ate much more casually. My granddad Ted taught me how to drink soup properly by angling the soup spoon towards the back of the dish and scooping the soup to then sip it gracefully. Maybe that's why I love soup so much!

However, back to those Sunday teas and a table with plenty of food every time we went. I remember the trifles, sandwiches, tinned fruit and evaporated milk.

And there was another tradition or ritual established, too, and that was around the celebrating of Christmas. We never visited on Christmas Day, and neither did they visit us! Even though Mum was their only child and Dad's family lived miles away, we all had Christmas Days behind closed doors.

Nan would arrange to have her Christmas Day for all of us at a different time. Within a few days but at a different time.

And now, looking back and thinking about it, the ritual was that we came together to celebrate Christmas on a day that was decided on and convenient to all. This seems, to my mind, to have the essence of rituals for festivals.

Do you have a family ritual which has been handed down, or perhaps you're creating one?

finding purpose

When we're feeling lost and bobbing around in the ocean with no compass or sail for our boat, it's crucial that we have a few emergency measures to call on.

Choose one of mine from here or maybe you have your own:

1. Place your hands over your heart and gently say, 'I come back to me'.
2. Prepare one item ready for the thrift shop. Thrift/charity shops are the ultimate for recycling, as whatever we donate will be used.
3. Go outside, place your hands on earth and say 'thank you'.
4. Wash a dish and see it shine in the light.
5. Walk in nature and feel the earth beneath your feet, the moisture in the air and the warmth from the Sun.

our story of us

In order to find our next part of the story, sometimes we need to take a moment out of time in whatever way makes sense to us as individuals and unique human beings.

To find our own golden thread to lead us forward.

To make our own ritual and acknowledge a special moment of processing is taking place - and reward ourselves ... with cake perhaps!

We have a rich source of information, not always in the language of words it has to be said, but available from around us and from our history.

And time is not always linear. At other points in this book, you will, if you choose to, experiment with seeing into other realms, hearing sounds that are beyond normal human perception, touch an object in order to tune in and sense it has history and expand taste and the sense of smell. During the grounding practises and visualisations, you may well step outside time and be surprised by how much, or how little, time by the clock has passed. There is so much more to our human existence than the 'here and now' … or rather,

***There is more to the 'here and now' of
our human existence!***

winter

Winter Solstice /
Yule

Halloween/
Samhain

Imbolc

Autumn Equinox /
Harvest

Spring Equinox /
Ostara

Lammas /
Harvest

Beltane /
May Day

Summer Solstice /
Midsummer

winter - november & december

The two dates of October 31st and November 1st have become, probably, the most celebrated individual dates of the whole of our wheel of the year and calendar. Halloween, or All Hallows Eve, as the night before All Souls Day, has such symbolism, history and mythology surrounding it that there could probably be a book all about just that one date!

One of the oddest legends I read for Halloween is that we shouldn't leave any clothes out to dry on the line outside because they could become infused with spirits. Presumably, the spirits are walking around looking for clothes to wear! But it is a time to protect our plants in the garden, to clear leaves and to bring fruit in. So perhaps there is the deeper significance of this time, and that is of protecting ourselves and our gardens ready for the coming Winter months by wearing all of our clothes!

Halloween begins the next turn of our wheel of the year, and so the Winter season of our eighth begins with the turn of November into December.

grounding & connecting

As we're in the darkest part of the year, maybe not the coldest but certainly the deepest time, we are invited to go inside and within. Our connection with the earth may seem like something that doesn't belong, and we may feel detached from the outside world. We will be limiting our ventures outdoors, and our world revolves around the indoors and those whom we have and will, over the next few weeks, be surrounded with - our nearest and dearest.

However, it is still as important for our sense of balance, and the essential part of the 'who' we are, that we connect and centre ourselves each day. Maybe more so!

Take a moment to sense where you are by standing (or sitting) still and reach your awareness down through your tailbone to the ground beneath and then further down until you sense the centre of the Earth.

Connect to the Earth.

And then expand your awareness out above the ceiling to the sky above your head and the infinity of the universe and space.

Connected to the Earth and the Universe.

Tune your frequency into the Earth and the Universe. Any sounds from the physical world around you are a part of life and to be celebrated, and then move your attention past them.

Feel the horizon of our planet stretching out from either side of you and in front and behind and all around you. Your light shines out to all the compass points and is even brighter in this time, for the Northern hemisphere, of the dark.

On the opposite side of the world, the sun shines brightly, and it is the lightest part of the year - Beltane.

All is in balance, and as you are at one with the earth, you feel strong in all directions.

Reinforce your bubble of light all around you and know that you are at one with your body and the body of the earth and universe.

Raise your hands up to the sky and then slowly take them down to touch the floor - or the earth if you are able to do this outside!

Stand up straight and tall, and be proud of the wonderful human you are.

And now you are grounded, tuned in to your own connected frequency of the Universe itself and ready to be human on this home planet of ours!!

samhain / halloween

Samhain is the ancient Celtic festival of the dead when bonfires were lit, and the ancestors remembered and celebrated. Exactly when it began to be known as Halloween, All Hallows Eve, is uncertain; however, the intentions of this time remained the same. October 31st is the evening for remembering those who have gone before, and then November 1st in celebration of them.

It's also a time when taxes will have been settled, so our ancestors would have taken stock of what was left to see them through. Twice a year, usually during Spring and after harvest, a portion of what had been grown or produced, whether money or goods, was paid to the landowner. Perhaps this was the origin of the whole notion of trick or treat. Are you the person being treated to extra money and goods, or did you have to pay a tithe and, as a result, have restricted rations?

Early Winter was a time when the Lords would release their soldiers to go back to their families. It's rare to find battles being fought in the depths of Winter, and the weather had to be such that the soldiers could travel. And so this would be the last time in the calendar that people really could move around easily, and families get together to see the cold months out under one roof.

Sometimes, we see this time at the end of October and the beginning of November as the Old Year becoming New Year. And that's why it's so symbolic for all of us to be thinking about what we want to take forward with us and what we want to leave and transform into something else. All around us, the Earth is decomposing, and whilst we might sweep up leaves, mostly in fields and woodland, the earth is taking delight in covering itself with a layer of old leaves, bark and whatever else may be breaking down to offer nutrients to the soil below.

> **The nature of decomposition is that it transforms into something else.**

Winter begins, colours fade, and the trees lose their foliage with only the green of evergreens remaining.

It's also a great feast time when things are never quite as they seem. The veil between realms is at its thinnest with messages received from ancestors.

Medieval Mystery Plays were often performed now with roles reversed and black and white clothes worn. With faces also painted half black and half white, identities were obscured, and it was the nature of the play, and the messages within that mattered rather than appearances.

It's time for another part of my story!

Growing up, I was quiet and could have won awards for the amount of daydreaming and retreating into the inner world that took place inside my brain every day. There are a myriad of reasons why I withdrew so much, and some are painful memories.

But I was the shy girl in the corner of the playground longing for friends and yet also terrified that someone, anyone, would actually talk to me.

Being born in August made me a Leo star sign - the one sign of the Zodiac that loves the limelight ... but not me!

And I tried - even joined a dramatic society. I took a speaking role or two, and they weren't too bad. But I really loved doing make-up, wardrobe, prompt ...

I couldn't possibly be a Leo - not when I read the stars in magazines.

In my corporate career, I gave induction talks and trained 100s of people in health and safety - so maybe there was my Leo! And in the early 90s, my astrological chart was set up and described to me by an astrologer.

The clouds parted, angels sang, and, for the first time, 'I' made sense!

The Sun was in Leo at the time of my birth and in a part of the horizon that loves delivering a message. The planets immediately next to the Sun at that moment are all geared up to help find ways for others to shine. No wonder I love to teach and train.

Knowing my birth chart saved me as, along with the joys, I understood how deeply I can be wounded. And since then, I have studied and learnt astrology for myself and to help others. From the beginning of my astro path, I went out and read the charts, and also tarot cards, for people all over the UK at camps and festivals. Hundreds and hundreds of charts and questions, and I love every one presented to me.

A birth chart is a living and breathing map of wonderful choices and opportunities to shine. A chart is of a unique moment in time. It can be for a person's birth, a business beginning or an event. And the information is ready and waiting for the unique experience of great choices.

You are your star/sun sign. And perfectly unique. You were born with all of the stars and planets around you in the zodiac. And so you are beautifully aligned for your own path here.

And now, back to Samhain and the Mystery plays that are often found around this time.

I took part in one before I knew about my birth chart. I loved it, and I wonder if you can tell why!!

There was a local competition for playwriters and actors, and somehow, I was recruited into a theatre company to enact one of the winning scripts. There were three of us out on the streets of Norwich performing the play in various locations. It was a part of the Lord Mayor's Procession Day in the early 1980s and so probably during July, and I suspect the original Mystery plays would have been held indoors if in the colder months!

Interestingly enough, the playwright I knew as Pete Green of Norwich, who wrote our play, was an astrologer, and our paths crossed many times after this as he organised Mind, body & spirit fairs at which I often had a table to read Tarot or astrology charts. He was also featured in a TV program called 'Busman's Holiday' as part of a team of astrologers, which included my dearest friend and mentor Joyce Collin-Smith - before I met her. Odd how these pathways of ours join up with significance!

festivals & 'ho' to the sun

And there are other similar festivals all around this time too. In the UK, we have Remembrance Day on November 11th and, in the USA, Thanksgiving on the 22nd. There are more all over the world around this time for this sense of remembering, and they are all usually fire festivals with bonfires or candles featuring.

In more recent times, we celebrate November 5th with bonfires and fireworks and, whilst this acknowledges the plot to blow up the Houses of Parliament in London with resulting executions and changes in laws, that we still use the date for the lighting of fires would suggest that there is a deeper ancestral memory at work here. Throughout history, we have seen the lighting of fires and candles as a symbolic gesture to ask for the Sun to return or to thank the Sun for warmth and life.

sleep, dreams & moon

As we are in the time of lengthier dark nights and entering colder weather, our sleep patterns may well change. There is a saying, 'rise with the larks,' and, before electric lights and when candles either cost money or took time to make, there is wisdom in making the best use of daylight hours. Our bodies react to daylight in a way very different to any other artificial light, so perhaps there is a real rhythm to remember here as well.

Often, sleep will alter with the cycles of the Moon, and many people find it impossible to sleep during a full moon. A theory of mine is that the full moon brought extra hours of light in which work could still be done, and this may well linger in our ancestral memories. And also, of course, there is extra gravitational pull at a Full Moon when the water table is high and energy at its most optimum for growth.

This seems a good place to turn our thoughts to the 'how' we sleep because there are different parts to how we sleep.

Sleep is a different form of consciousness to awake and also different to meditation, daydreaming, induced coma or any other way we have of being in an altered state of being. Sleep is a natural form of rest for us all and also has several different stages.

Hypnagogia and Hypnopompia

Hypnagogia is the state of being when we are on the verge of falling asleep, and hypnopompia is just as we are about to wake. During those two times, we often dream, or we'll have random thoughts, or we'll get insights. It's a different state of being. And when we don't think that we're sleeping, often we're in a different state. We may not be fully awake. But we're in a different state. And at certain times, particularly during the dark of the moon before the New, I believe we have more access to the different states of consciousness. Is this useful knowledge? I believe so, as we can take notice of those thoughts we have on waking or the dreams and see whether there is a pattern or a nudge from our intuition.

It's worth noting what your sleep is like because it does change according to the Moon and also the cycle of the year. And thinking of the Moon here, we know that her energy really does affect our insights and emotions.

As part of your own research into 'you,' it may well be useful to keep a note of the different states of sleep and when dreams happen. The subject of dreaming and particularly lucid dreams probably belongs in another book to this one; however, November and December are dark months when we can, perhaps, access a different part of our own consciousness, especially if we are determining what our real-life theme type dreams are to be for the coming Yule time!

notes from the ancestors

I sat with the ancestors for this segment of the book. And asked who would step forward for Samhain. It was Grandad Ted who brought this memory forward.

> *He once told me that the richest people he had met were not the wealthiest.*

Grandad Ted would decide on the seeds he wanted to buy or acquire in December. He would begin to plan his garden and cover the earth with compost. Never one to let the larder be empty, there would still be winter vegetables to be harvested, and Nan would still be creating food and pickling anything that wasn't going to be eaten immediately.

The cycle of Nature isn't a calendar even though I've attempted, in this book, to give a structure to our 'year'. Our calendars need that leap year day, and our moon watching will never be regular, according to our diaries.

Cycles and rhythms.

Grandad Ted knew the cycles and rhythms and, through that, enabled our lives to be so much richer.

And so, on the subject of wealth. Health would feature. Love and kindness to one another. Generosity and love … oh … I already said that one! What features are in your 'wealth list'?

being

Pumpkins and turnips. Trees losing their leaves and colour. Nature is changing all around us, and it is time for us to alter our living spaces.

What can you do over the next few weeks to make indoors cosy and welcoming? To both expand the living space whilst ensuring you'll be warm. To have your own cauldron bubbling away of a stew or soup ... root vegetables will, quite literally, help us stay warm, full and grounded.

Use the nudges from nature and from our deep ancestral memories to bring the sense of love into our homes. This will be your base camp for the next few months, so how do you feel when you walk in through the front door, and how can you make it feel even more 'yours'?

We are now entering a time of year when the elements, especially cold air and rain, will be more keenly felt by us and, symbolically, we can prepare ourselves. Place something representing each one onto a shelf and glance at them from time to time.

We are made from stardust
and yet born onto planet Earth …

- **Air** - a feather, incense, fan or something pale blue
- **Earth** - a leaf, a stone or something green or brown
- **Water** - a dish, a bottle or something deep blue
- **Fire** - a candle (unlit), a match or something red or orange

doing

We first met the subject of scrying in our February chapter when welcoming in Imbolc energy. Throughout the book, we have looked at different ways of accessing our inner language, and there are another couple in the 'Playing' section of this chapter!

And so I thought a few ways of beginning divination would work here too ... it is, after all, a time when we know the airwaves are busy with messages from 'beyond'!

Scrying creates a means for the brain to switch off and for our imagination to operate at full pelt. There is magic in our imagination, and we only need to give it space and to listen or, watch or feel.

A quick and easy way of scrying is to put a few drops of black ink or paint into a bowl of water, peer in, and let your mind drift. What do you see, hear, feel - remember, we are using our ordinary senses in a different way and one in which they expand. And this may take practice, too!

If you are able to walk outside at this time of the year, the trees are still living and breathing and have messages to share. Connect your inner landscape with the outer by walking and just gently asking what you could do with knowing today! You may be surprised by just what happens after your return to base!

And then there are the Tarot and also Runes - both of these systems of listening to the intuition are just that ... a way into your own inner world where you already know so much more than you remember in your daily existence!

playing

It's time to weave some stories and tell tales from times gone past. Creating fairy tales and mythic adventures not only while away long evenings spent around the fire but also pass on memories and history.

During these evenings when the nights are longer, and the weather outside is cold, could you write magical stories where the heroines rule the world, or cats chase dogs, or there is no concept of money or ... I'll leave it to you to write the unexpected with nothing being quite as it would appear to be at first glance.

Our ancestors loved tales of a cauldron of everlasting food and the stranger knocking at the door with exciting news ...

Begin to dream of what you will weave as stories or as cloth. Or even make yourself a mask to hide your identity from any spirits who dare to lurk!

stillness

To welcome our ancestors and our guides. Place an extra setting at the table and light your candle in the window. Quietly say that your home is open to kind and loving friends and family members who wish to visit.

Eat the meal with laughter and joy and then wash the dishes as if all of them had been used.

Maybe your message from an ancestor or guide will be heard, felt, sensed or come later!

Old Year & New Year.

The movement of the Earth, Sun and Moon is full of rhythm and cycles, and, as we've already seen, nothing ever stops in the

Universe of ours. However, this next thought process can be stronger at this time particularly!

Just close your eyes for a moment and remember what you've gathered up over these past few months. Maybe you planted something and harvested it. Did a Springtime intention become a reality or a memory?

Visualise a symbol for Spring (anything that comes to mind is perfect!)

Visualise a symbol for Summer.

Visualise a symbol for Autumn.

Visualise a symbol for Winter.

And then sit silently at peace with the year.

There is nothing more to do than just acknowledge the symbols or thoughts or even nothingness that appears during this time!

Remind yourself (use a timer, perhaps) to return to the room and ground yourself.

Take some time to write or doodle your thoughts and insights.

We are in the darkest months, so you really can take your time with this inner landscape musing!

dear friend

Dear Friend,

We know each other, you and I. We've walked the seasons of the year and matched our personal rhythm to that of the Earth and our amazing Universe. Of course, we've done it in different ways, learnt and played with energies and time, been to special places in our minds and with our bodies, and used our own unique compasses to set our pathways in place. And it's a never-ending journey as the world, our world, continually turns and the seasons unfold and move from one to the next.

Where did you begin?

Where will you go next?

I wish for you

As your personal connection with earth energies deepens

And the seasons unfold in beauty & grace around you

Yule returns the light

Little Spring brings hope

Spring offers growth

Little Summer adds colour

Summer ripens wisdom

Harvest realises gifts

Autumn presents bounty

Samhain observes continuance

Yule returns the light

And remember to take a moment out of time as needed!

As always, with love from Alison

acknowledgments

Thank you to my amazing Husband, Terry, who loves and supports me on this crazy roller-coaster of our lives in this lifetime.

Thank you to my publishers, who have pulled this book out of me from deep inside. Karen, your mentorship, beautiful skill for editing and kindness goes beyond. And Sean ... when we first met so briefly years ago, we couldn't have envisioned how that connection would lead to ... well ... this!

Thank you to my two amazing friends who became family and were both called Joyce and to Rainbow Circle - all of you lifted me up, loved and inspired me along the way. As have other dear friends too - you know who you are!

Thank you to Spirit, Nature, Earth and the realms around us in which I walk every day alongside you all.

Which, of course, brings me to say a big thank you to you for reading and, I hope, 'Being, Doing, Playing & finding ways of Stillness' through this book.

about the author

Alison Smith is a professional astrologer, intuitive, tarot reader & earth energies explorer of more than 30 years. She is known for her practical interpretations and the 'how can we use this' approach to our life in this Universe.

Her website is www.alisontheastrologer.com, and you can also find her on social media by searching for Alison Smith Practical Astrology.

Alison now teaches the extraordinary ways our intuition can unveil so much about earth energies and planetary energies and, of course, ourselves! With decades of professional experience giving readings, workshops, courses and walking her talk, she has been featured in magazines for weekly horoscopes and the national press for Royal event articles, and this is her third book in print.

Her passion is to simplify the alchemical mix of astrology, earth energies, tarot and intuition for the manifestation of the best choices! And that passion expands into being aware of our crucial roles as stewards of Earth. Recently, Alison has been a part of the regenerative textiles movement exploring slow-growing fibres.

Currently living in North Wales, Alison loves to go to festivals in a camper van and to listen to live music. And she weaves wool and stories and loves cake!

Printed in Great Britain
by Amazon

36729197R00212